Revive!

?2

Revive!

Inspired Interiors from Recycled Materials

Jacqueline Mulvaney

A&C Black • London

First published in Great Britain in 2010
A & C Black Publishers Limited
36 Soho Square
London W1D 3QY
www.acblack.com

ISBN 978-1-408-10627-3

CIP Catalogue records for this book are available from the British Library.

Book design by Penny Mills.
Cover design by Sutchinda Thompson.
Commissioned by Alison Stace.

Printed and bound in Singapore.

This book is produced using paper that is made from wood grown in
managed, sustainable forests. It is natural, renewable and recyclable. The
logging and manufacturing processes conform to the environmental
regulations of the country of origin.

Acknowledgements

Thanks go to my mum for thinking it's lovely.
Special thanks go to Deborah and Philip Challinor.

Contents

Introduction

WHETHER WE REALISE it or not we all collect textiles. Most of us only have to take a quick look in the wardrobe to know we are not good at disposing of surplus clothes. Then there are the items we treasure: the wedding dress, the party dress, baby clothes long outgrown. We may occasionally have a clear-out, bag up these items and hand them to charity shops or sell them for peanuts (later regretted) at sales or via the internet. This book aims to make you look at textiles in a more creative way, and asks you to be more imaginative when you view the slightly shabby and no longer fashionable. I want you to develop a horror at the thought of wasting serviceable, often very beautiful, fabric. I hope you will be inspired to create beautiful objects that you will use and love, working exclusively with fabrics you already possess or can source with ease.

The projects will start gently. The only assumption will be that you have a basic knowledge of sewing and a real passion to learn more. As the projects progress the level of complexity will increase, but I hope always to include alternative suggestions or tips to make your work easier and help develop your confidence. Don't be afraid to go 'off piste' and try your own thing. Think of this book as a series of recipes which you can adapt to suit your individual taste. You have to have fun too.

Although some of these projects are simple, please consider them precious. Don't rush. Spend some time considering fabric choices, trimmings and decoration. Enjoy the making process and take pleasure in seeing something wonderful develop. You will want to use the final pieces so make them well. Like good, slow cooking, let the flavours develop!

BELOW AND DETAIL LEFT: Billy's cushion. Reclaimed linen, silk and cotton. Embroidered and embellished with buttons and military medal.

1 Getting Started

Ithink this is the most exciting part of any project, finding inspiration through sourcing fabrics, gathering ideas and working out your chosen project. If you want to make a quality product, a piece that you will cherish and want to use, then spending time thinking and preparing is time well spent.

All projects begin with your materials. While visiting your local fabric shop and making friends with the owner is a good idea, and should result in off-cuts and end-of-roll bargains, concentrate on what you already own, or what's available from friends or local charity shops. I have friends and family who are more than happy to pass over generous bundles of clothing that are no longer serviceable or fashionable. One particular donor uses me to thin out her wardrobe simply so that she can buy

more! However I acquire these gems they are always gratefully received. As my nieces have grown their pretty dresses and printed shirts have all found their way into cushions and throws. It's worth noting that children's clothes often contain substantial amounts of trim and fastenings, so it's useful to spending time deconstructing these garments, as decorative trimmings are often the most expensive textiles to purchase. Let your friends know that you want first look at any potential cast-offs.

Although charity shops can be a bit hit and miss, the thrill is in the hunt. I visit two or three shops regularly; the staff are incredibly helpful and seem delighted if they manage to find me a real gem. I have to stress that these shops are best for finding everyday textiles: old curtains, dresses, skirts and shirts. These items will provide quantity, not necessarily the most decorative or beautiful fabrics, but as we shall see later it's what is done to these surfaces that render them desirable.

Obviously, one of the prime reasons to use charity shops is thrift. An awful lot of material can be purchased for the equivalent of a metre (yard) of new fabric. The trick is to spot the potential of second-hand garments. I confess I didn't like handling other people's cast-offs at first, but now I have learnt what rich rewards can be gained from a rummage in a well-stocked charity shop. The items have usually been cleaned and pressed, so the only hard work is cutting the fabric into usable sections.

I must also sing the praises of flea markets and vintage textile fairs which never fail to yield a good stash of fabric and haberdashery. We have a

LEFT AND OPPOSITE: Recycled fabrics. Box of buttons. Trims. Equipment.
TOP AND MIDDLE LEFT: Details of stitch on finished items.

monthly market in our local town, and in addition to the china, glass and cutlery there are several stalls selling textiles such as old tablecloths, napkins and tray cloths. All these items are beautifully laundered and trimmed with lace and faded embroidery. While not 'vintage', and possessing little intrinsic value, these pieces make fabulous cushions, sections of throws or quirky tea cosies. Again, attending these events regularly is key, as you can strike up a relationship with the stall-holders who will get to know your requirements.

I recommend visiting the specialist vintage textile fairs, not just to purchase but to gain inspiration. I live near Bath, where a textile fair takes place twice yearly at the Assembly Rooms. There are a huge range of vendors there, from expensive retailers of antique costumes to sellers of affordable, fun items that cost very little but will give your work an individual quality. I love French domestic textiles, particularly tea cloths, table napkins and linen roller towels; not particularly prepossessing in themselves but wonderful fabrics to work with. (See p.94 for a list of textile events.)

Of course you don't have to be passionate about textiles to care about recycling and sustainability. Creating beautiful objects from used or discarded items is a splendid way of turning our backs on the mass-produced and working towards a sustainable approach to consumerism. This is not hair-shirt rhetoric, just a desire to work with the unique and to live with beautiful objects.

Preparing your finds

It is important to discuss how to prepare your finds for the projects that follow. Let's assume you have plundered friends and family and raided your local charity shop: you are now sitting looking at a pile of rather sad-looking items. Old clothes can look a little dispiriting when heaped untidily on the floor. Make a cup of tea and sit and look for a while.

Start by sorting your stash by type. Spend time taking clothing to pieces. Separate buttons and trims from the main fabric and then cut into usable sections. If your fabric is mostly clothing then go for shirts in one pile, dresses in another, and so on. At this stage don't worry about what colour items are, what sort of fabric, etc. You will now need your scissors and a seam

ABOVE: Deconstructing fabrics. **OPPOSITE:** Detail of stitch on finished item.

ripper. Look carefully at what you have. Begin by taking off any fastenings and store in a separate container. If an item has buttonholes cut them off and keep them, as they can be reused when buttons are required, and will save you having to construct new holes.

Does your item have any decorative trim? If so, cut it off carefully, roll it into a skein and store separately. I know this sounds a bit prim, but if you stuff a bag full of bits of trim, fastenings and fabric off-cuts finding exactly what you need becomes impossible. Also, messy bags of unidentified pieces aren't special, they won't inspire you, and you'll be very likely to throw them away. Start to form good storage habits.

Once you have removed all the extraneous items consider what is left. Try and imagine what the item might be used for, not specifically but in general terms: is it going to be a cushion, part of a curtain, a section of a throw? Obviously, a lot depends on the size of the garment – always look for clothes in the larger sizes as there is much more fabric involved. Try and unpick seams where you can rather than merely cutting off sections. This is more time-

consuming, but will result in larger sections of fabric. It could be that you have an item where the quantity of fabric is of little importance; you just want a particular section of embroidery or pattern. Take care removing what you want, but don't throw the rest away. Always keep remnants – you never know when the unwanted will become the

desperately needed.

With domestic textiles such as curtains or tablecloths, check for wear and tear. Faded fabric can still be gorgeous, rips can be repaired, and even stained fabric can be rescued by dyeing. You will learn when a piece of fabric is beyond the pale, only fit for dusters or the bin. If you do have fabric that needs

to be dyed, collect enough to make it worthwhile. You need to develop an eye for future projects. You may not intend to make new curtains in the immediate future, but that time might arrive, so again, preserve and conserve. I always compare the process of fabric deconstruction to making a good stock: you are removing the remains of the meat and then simmering the carcass which will provide you with the base for several delicious meals.

Grading and sorting

After a couple of hours of happy cutting and folding, consider what you have. This is the time to begin grading and sorting your treasure. It's up to you how you organise the material, but please consider buying a few boxes or baskets to contain the different kinds of fabric. You can then see what you have.

I like to sort my fabric into types in terms of cottons, linens, silks, and then into colour ranges, printed and plains. You may well have better things to do with

ABOVE: Grade and store your fabric.
LEFT: Fabrics ready and waiting to be reborn as something new.

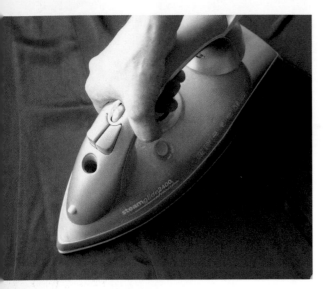

Clean and press fabric.

your life, but feel free to sub-divide to your heart's content! You don't have to iron everything, but a lot of second-hand items will need some tender ministrations, so be prepared for some laundry. Washing and ironing fabric at this point saves a lot of time later when you are keen to start making. Sort out your fabric into different types, weights and colours. Try and store them so that they are visible and easily accessed. It's always best to do these chores before getting excited about a project when all you want to do is make. I may well be stating the obvious with this information, but sometimes it's little hints and tips that make life so much easier later on.

Equipment

You now have to consider what equipment you will need. Obviously, you require space to work. You don't need a full-blown studio, or even a separate room, but it's easier if you can create a space that is yours, if only at certain times of the day. You will need a good, constant light source: stitching in poor light is little fun and frankly dangerous. Find somewhere you can be quiet, if possible a room where you can shut the door. Think about the sort of project you want to complete and how long it might take. If you can commandeer an area where it's feasible to leave work in mid-project so much the better. Fundamentally though, there is nothing wrong with the good old kitchen table.

Sewing machines

I have written this book based on the premise that readers own a sewing machine and know how to use it. I will go into some detail regarding certain stitch methods, and if your machine is different to mine you will need to consult your manual, but most of

what I demonstrate is easily achievable irrespective of what type of machine you own. You will need a zig-zag foot and in some instances a freehand embroidery foot. The embroidery foot is usually sold separately to the sewing machine and it is worth investing in one.

At this point it's important to go into more detail regarding your machine. I own a Bernina 1008; if you have any experience of art college or sewing classes you may well be familiar with this particular model. It is semi-industrial and will take a lot of abuse. I have seen students do unspeakable things to these machines and they still chug into action. If you are going to be stitching regularly, then I do recommend you invest in a basic, tough model. I don't own a machine that is computerised, as everything I make is dependent on machine embroidery and straightforward stitches. You will probably have your own allegiances, but don't feel you have to buy an all-singing, all-dancing machine immediately. I do advise

My studio. Nothing fancy, in fact a small space, but it's light, quiet and mine!

finding a good retailer. I bought my machine from a tiny shop in a local market town and they were fantastic. I got good service, but more important a huge amount of excellent technical knowledge and efficient aftercare. You do need to have your machine serviced regularly, and I would suggest you change your needle regularly, and learn how to do basic maintenance, such as oiling.

When you have settled on the right model for you, please spend some time reading the manual. I know it's tempting to just start sewing, but you will get more from the machine if you understand what it can and can't do. Also, keep the instruction book

with your machine – most glitches can be solved by you and won't require professional intervention. (When my machine arrived I took it to pieces before I used it. Not necessarily something you should do but it helped me understand what made it tick.)

Machine accessories

Check out what equipment comes as standard with your model. All machines should have a presser foot (which holds the fabric in place while you stitch it), that does straight and zig-zag stitch, and in addition there are usually buttonhole, zipper, overlock and blind-stitch presser feet; you can

also buy embroidery feet.

For the purposes of this book, you will only need the standard presser foot (which comes with the machine) and an embroidery foot (which you will need to buy separately). As you progress and begin to be more experimental and creative you might want to buy specialist feet. Some will need to be ordered from your local haberdashery store or from online stores. (See Suppliers List p.94) I bought a freehand embroidery foot with my machine and I couldn't do without it. It has a circular needle opening which enables me to have an unobstructed view of what I am working on. I tend to use this and the zig-zag foot almost exclusively. For some of the projects in this book you will need an embroidery foot, and when we reach the projects I will go into more detail on how to use it.

To progress on beyond this book I would also recommend a couching foot (for securing cords and braids to fabric), tailor tack foot (producing tufted stitch for decorative use) and pintuck foot (used with a twin needle to create pin tucks). You don't need them for the projects in this

My sewing machine: after my husband and dog this is the item I would rescue from a burning house. Love it and it will love you.

Pins, needles, threads, scissors, tape measure, straight edge, fabric adhesive and embroidery hoop. Minor equipment but essential for all these projects.

book, but they are good to have as you become more proficient and experimental. Don't buy these items all at once, as you won't need them immediately, so treat yourself as you progress.

Minor equipment

A good selection of threads is not merely a luxury. You will need cotton threads and embroidery (polyester) threads. There is a dizzying array of colours available, plus metallic and multi-coloured threads.

Go to your local haberdashery and get a feel for the types and colours that suit you. If you don't live near a decent shop, there are some very good online stores (see p.94 for suppliers). For general seam stitching cotton or cotton-covered polyester thread is fine. If the stitch is on show or decorative then machine embroidery thread might be desirable: these threads have a lovely sheen and give weight and lustre to your work.

You will need a selection of machine needles, as you

probably have a variety of fabric weights to work with. Machine needles are generally sold in packets and are graded in terms of size, for example: 10/70 needle for medium-weight fabric. All packets are labelled with size and fabric suitability. A packet of machine embroidery needles will also be useful. Hand-sewing needles will be required for some projects: sharps with a small eye for general sewing, embroidery needles with larger eyes for thicker threads, and beading needles which are extra fine to enable them to go through bead holes. A couple of varieties of pins, including household and dressmaking, will also be needed. None of these items are expensive and once you have invested in them you will be set up for a while.

A cutting mat is invaluable, especially if you are working on a good table that you would prefer to remain unmarked. If you can invest in an A1 size mat so much the better. You will also need a metal rule and a tape measure.

It goes without saying that quality scissors are a must. Fabric scissors are for fabrics only, not for cutting paper, plastic, metal or anything else (I'm thinking of indiscretions committed by my husband here). A pair of all-purpose shears is useful as are small, sharp embroidery scissors. I have recently invested in a rotary cutter, which I love; it is fabulously sharp and enables you to cut layers of fabric with ease. You might find one useful if you are going to cut large quantities of fabric often.

I always have a couple of types of adhesive on hand, a PVA, and a waterproof textile glue. Sometimes you want to secure decorations before stitching, or simply want to use glue rather than stitch. Look for products that are specifically for textile use and can be washed. These products are quick-drying and easy to use, but be sure to use in a well-ventilated space.

Other equipment you might need includes: a medium-size embroidery hoop, fabric stabiliser such as 'stitch and tear', a few artist's paintbrushes and a basic toolkit: hammer, panel pins, upholstery tacks and screwdriver.

Inspiration

Having discussed equipment and all things practical, let's think about what's most important: inspiration. Try to keep a journal to record imagery that you might find useful. Don't worry about beautiful drawings; go for found imagery, rubbings to record textures and cuttings from magazines. Enjoy yourself. With luck you will be inspired by your collection of fabrics and the potential they offer, but the key to producing beautiful objects is a great idea or starting point. I have always kept a sketchbook and I would urge you to develop the habit. Sketchbooks are personal interpretations of your visual language, i.e. where you put all your ideas. I carry mine with me everywhere, so it is just as likely to contain shopping lists as it does images, thoughts and magazine cuttings. It does not have to be beautiful but like children we always think ours are the nicest! Don't buy a huge, heavy book, just something that fits into your bag, is hard-backed and contains reasonable quality paper. Don't be shy; you don't have to show the sketchbook to anyone – it's personal. An ability to draw is not required; some of the most delightful journals are collections of found imagery, text and colour. There are so many times we see something wonderful but fail to record it; even if all you do is describe what excited you, that moment will not be lost. You will soon come to rely on its contents. If you do start a sketchbook, try developing a theme to your ideas that you can then translate into the projects you tackle. Having a visual resource is like being able to consult a recipe book, one that informs creatively and helps you out of a rut.

I think using a camera is a brilliant way to extend your visual imagery, especially if you can link your camera to a computer and review pictures on screen. I don't create images using computers but if you do, then feel free to produce starting points in this way: anything to get you thinking laterally and more creatively.

Finally, I would suggest that if you have the time, enjoy doing some research: see some exhibitions, visit a beautiful place or buy a lush book. I used to tell students who said they didn't like research that my favourite method of gaining useful information was lying in the bath with a glass of wine, reading *Vogue*. I'm still a big fan of that.

Pinboard and sketchbook. A glimpse at some of my sources of Inspiration, showing my personal interpretation of what makes me excited.

2 Cushions

A BIG MOUND OF SILK cushions complete with fringes, sequins and trims is my idea of heaven. A thing of beauty, but also functional; lovely to cuddle up to but also very useful to cover up a tired sofa. But considering the quite basic designs that are commercially available cushions are often prohibitively expensive. Fortunately, cushion making is easy, with simple shapes and very few pieces. A basic shape can be completed in less than an hour; what happens next is where the excitement lies.

Before you begin, decide on a few basics. Where is your cushion going to be used? What size do you want to make? Indoor or outdoor use? Colours, shape, texture? What feel of fabric do you want? If you take time to consider some of these questions before you begin to cut and sew you will produce a more satisfying end product, one that will give you pleasure and last a long time.

I like to have lots of colours and shapes juxtaposed. You may well prefer a cooler, more neutral palette. You might want to make a quick mood board to guide and inspire you. A mood board can be no more than a table on which you arrange fabric, trims and threads. Try and work out what you want to use in advance so that you can narrow down your collection and get your fabrics to work together well. Move your chosen items around to achieve a balance of colour, fabric weight and texture. If it helps, cut small swatches of fabric and pin them in your sketchbook so you remember your thoughts. This is an optional stage, but it's surprising how narrowing down a big stack of fabric to a few carefully selected pieces makes for a stronger end result.

BELOW AND OPPOSITE: Examples of completed cushions.

To begin with I'll make a simple square floor cushion, taking the making process to the point where decoration can start. You can make your cushion as plain or fancy as you choose. Any added decoration shown is usable on any of the projects in this book: the corsage shown on p.28–9 would look equally striking on a throw or blind.

ABOVE: Fabrics and trims to be used in the cushion. Selecting a good combination of materials before starting will create a better cushion.
RIGHT: Equipment you will need for this project.

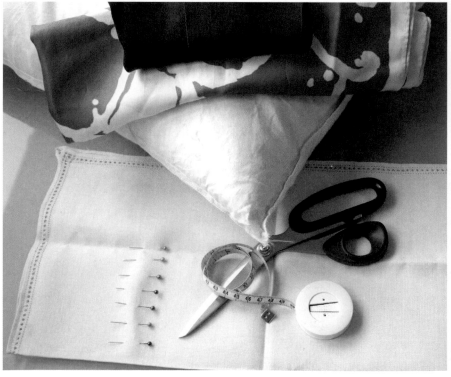

Equipment

Once you have considered what type of cushion you want to construct you will need to assemble the following equipment: fabric scissors, ruler, pins and threads. Don't feel that your threads have to match your fabric – seeing flashes of contrasting or even clashing colours is going to be part of your cushion's charm. Use cotton mix threads for sewing your pieces together, but change to embroidery threads for any more visible stitches.

Obviously, you need to have enough fabric to make

your cushion. Although the cushion I've chosen to make uses a larger piece of material, don't feel you have to always use single lengths of cloth. You can produce wonderful objects from much smaller scraps which can be pieced together to create bands of colour and texture. But if this is your first attempt at making a cushion, make your life easier and go for as few pieces as possible. This might make your work look a bit stark in the first instance, but it is then a blank canvas for your decorations. I have chosen a silk scarf for the front of my cushion and fabric from an old skirt for the reverse. Cutting and laying out your composition is important, so take time to experiment with different compositions and layouts before you begin.

I have selected a feather cushion pad which is 56cm (22in) square. I do think it's important to consider the different pads available. I prefer feather-filled cushions, as they

are durable and long-lasting, and I love plumping them up in the morning! Feather pads have soft cotton covers which work well under any fabric. The covers are almost always neutral coloured so if you are using a fine, lightweight fabric you may have to add a lining to prevent the cushion pad showing through. Square, rectangular and circular feather pads are widely available, but if you want a more unusual shape or a much larger size then bespoke pads can be ordered (see p.94 for details of suppliers).

If you don't want to use feather pads then man-made hollow fibre ones are just as easy to obtain. They hold their shape, but do not wear as well as feather ones and tend to go flat after a while. It's worth considering that cushions are used on a daily basis and have to survive children, adults and pets of all shapes and sizes, so a robust, well-made filling is essential.

A silk scarf and an old skirt for the cushion.

Cutting out and making up

Measure a square which is 1in (2.5cm) bigger on all sides than your cushion pad (image A). This will be the front. For this cushion I'm going to show you how to make a split opening. For the back cut a piece of fabric the same width as the front but longer by 5in (12cm). You need the extra length to enable the opening to overlap and not show the cushion pad.

Cut the fabric you are using for the back of the cushion into two pieces. These pieces can be equal in length or, if you wish, you can make the back from two different pieces of fabric and have one section longer than the other. This allows you to use up smaller quantities of material and, I think makes the back of the cushion more interesting. Before you put your cushion together, and using your sewing machine, stitch a 0.5cm (¼ in) hem on the opening sides of your backing fabric. This will prevent the edges fraying.

Once you have assembled the different sections, place your front and back pieces with the right sides together. (When you sew your pieces you work on the wrong side of the fabric.) Pin the pieces

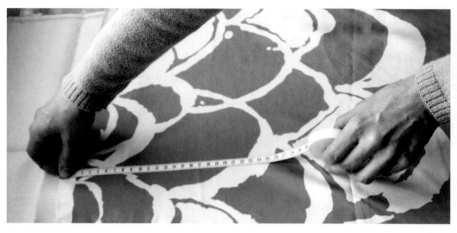

A Make sure you leave a hem allowance around the sides of the cushion.

B Placing a couple of pins in the centre of the cushion makes it easier to handle when stitching the components together.

C The two pieces of fabric should overlap each other in the centre.

together, placing your pins 2.5cm (1in) from the edges of the fabric. You may want to put a couple of pins in the centre too, to make the fabric easier to handle while stitching (image B). The two back halves will overlap each other in the middle making the seam a bit thicker. Using the sewing machine, stitch the sections to each other to form an inside-

out envelope. Use a medium-length straight stitch and follow your pins. Remove the pins as you sew. When you have completed the entire square, trim the excess fabric from the seam edges. Turn your work right side out and iron. Get into the habit of ironing your work as you complete important stages; this ensures a more professional finish.

Ribbon ties

Look at the back of your cushion. The two pieces of fabric should overlap so that an extra fastening should not be necessary (image C). However, you can add ribbon ties for extra security and decoration. Cut the ribbon to the length you require, turn one end over on itself and pin. Place one length of ribbon on the outer edge of the cushion opening. Make another tie in the same manner and place opposite the first piece. Hand stitch the ribbons onto the fabric so that they face each other. Feel free to add as many ties as you like (image D). Try using different coloured ribbons on each side of the opening. Stitch the ties on with contrasting coloured thread. You can also use large hooks and eyes or snap fastenings if you want. You can of course use a zip to fasten your cushion, I just think that the envelope method is more unusual and allows you to make the back as decorative as the front.

D Using ribbon ties creates a lovely soft closure for your cushion.

Decoration

You should check that your cushion pad fits before you go to town on any embellishments. Ease the pad into your cover, it should fit snugly. Leave the pad inside its new cover while you think about decoration. Much as making any new piece is satisfying, for me the fun starts when I can get going with decoration. I've always maintained that less is a bore and that a good cake always needs icing. If you are a more restrained creature then make yourself a series of elegant, unadorned cushions, but if you do like a good corsage, then carry on reading.

Corsage

Adding decoration that is blatantly three-dimensional to a functional piece can be tricky. You do want your cushion to be usable and cosy, so these instructions are for a flat floral trim. You will need a variety of fabric scraps: use pieces of material that work well with your cushion. Don't be shy. Think about contrasting colour, texture and weight of fabric and how they work with the overall piece. You will also require an A4 piece of thin card, pencil, general sewing thread, sewing needle, scissors, fabric adhesive and assorted buttons and beads. Try using buttons from reclaimed items if you can. It's quite useful at this point to produce a template shape for your flower petal. You can make a series of different shapes and sizes, cut them out and store them for future use. You should get quite a few from a single sheet of A4 card. Practice on a scrap of paper first, and then draw the type of petal you want (image A). I have drawn a double-ended shape (see opposite), overall length 8in (20cm), which saves you cutting out single pieces of fabric which have to be sewn together individually. Cut out at least 25 petals using

Materials you will need for your corsage.

A Make your petal shapes as elaborate as you like.

C Fabric glue is great for this type of work, it saves you from stitching each individual piece.

your chosen shape. You can layer your fabric, draw around your template on the top piece and then cut out several shapes together.

When you feel you have enough petals, spread them out, and then begin to assemble the flower. Place one petal on top of another but move it slightly clockwise so that your petals are individually visible (image B). Continue until you have used five or six of your pieces, then pin the centres together. Using your needle and thread stitch the assembled petals together through the centres only. It's nicer if the petals can be left

B Rotate your petal shapes to enable the colours and patterns in your fabric to show.

to do their own thing! Repeat this process until all your petals have been used. Otherwise use fabric adhesive (Bostik or Uhu are good fabric glue options) to attach the centres

of the flowers (image C).

The final piece will still be flat and soft, but should have plenty of interest in terms of colour and texture. Wait until the adhesive between the layers has dried then enjoy stitching your chosen buttons and beads into the centre of the flower.

Place your decoration on your cushion and play around with positioning it. Don't just put it in the centre! Depending on the dimensions of your flower decide if one will be sufficient or whether you want to make more. If you feel so inclined you could cover your entire cushion with different-sized decorations. Again, a lot depends on where your cushion is destined to spend its life. When you are satisfied

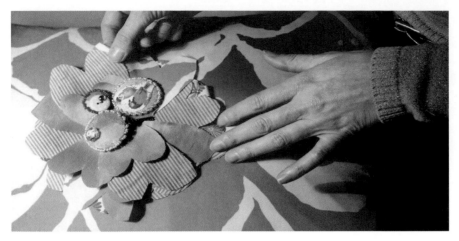

D Try moving the flower motif around before you settle on its final position.

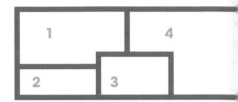

Stages

1 Materials required for tassel making.
2   Cut out your strips of fabric; be generous, you want your tassel to be lovely and fat!
3 You must secure the bundle of fabric tightly otherwise your tassel will shed its strips.
4 Use any spare pieces of trim or haberdashery that you think would work well with your tassel.

with the arrangement use adhesive to secure your flower in position (image D). Only use the glue on the reverse of the centre, you can then decide if you want the petals to remain loose and floppy or you could use tiny stitches to catch individual petals to the cushion cover. Feel free to continue the buttons across the surface of the cover.

Do try to develop the ability to evaluate what you make, not only in terms of its suitability but also its overall composition. Keep standing back and looking at how the piece is developing. Assuming you are happy with your efforts, give yourself a pat on the back and enjoy your new cushion.

You can use this chapter as a guide when trying other cushion shapes. Try making some larger pieces for the floor. If you have a garden, think about making some outdoor cushions. You will need to consider the type of fabric you choose – make the top from more robust material and the reverse from oil-cloth. You should still be able to find second-hand outdoor fabrics. I saw a fantastic mac in a charity shop recently and thought it would make a wonderful cushion for picnics. You could incorporate the belt and buttons into the final design for something a little more tongue in cheek.

ssels offer an extra
rish to cushions. You can use
m traditionally at the corners,
go your own way and add
m in lines across the cover or
them in the centre of flowers.
can easily use ready-
de tassels salvaged from
curtains or lampshades, but
se tend to be a little dull and
often be quite worn and
bby. In making your own you
produce something which
ks perfectly with your piece.

make a basic tassel you will
d scraps of your chosen
ric and some thin ribbon –
(50cm) will be more than

enough. **(Stage 1)** Cut lengths
of your fabric into strips of approximately 1cm (½ in) x 20cm
(8in). You will need a minimum
of 20, depending on how thick
you want your end product to be.
Lay your strips together, **(Stage 2)**,
then take half the length of your
fine ribbon and tie it tightly in the
middle of your bundle. Pick the
tied bunch of fabric up and fold
in half at the knot. Using the re-
maining length of ribbon wrap it
around the fabric approximately
2cm (¾ in) down from the knot.
Secure the ribbon with a dou-
ble knot **(Stage 3)**. You will now
have a simple tassel. The fabric
you have used will want to fray,

which is lovely, but to prevent too
much material loss you can tie
knots at the bottom of the strips
individually. Now you can have
fun customising your trimmings:
attach buttons, tie extra pieces of
ribbon to the tassel, and suspend
feathers from the fabric lengths
(Stage 4). You can make big,
fat tassels which are a feature
in themselves, or make a pile of
mini-tassels which you could sew
onto ribbon and use as an individual trim.

I hope you have enjoyed your
first foray into creative recycling
and are now ready to move
onto the next project.

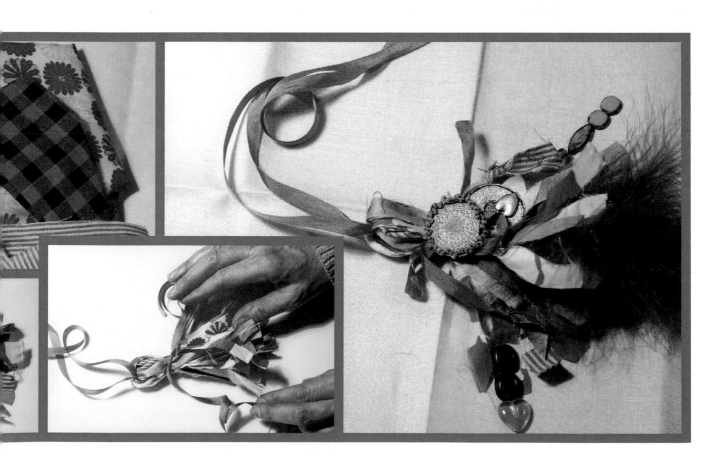

3 Throws

I n this chapter we are going to make a throw suitable for either a sofa or bed. It requires more fabric, but still uses quite basic sewing skills. Obviously, making a larger piece of work does take more confidence, as you need to think how your aesthetic decisions will look when scaled up.

Before you begin, spend some time researching examples that you find inspirational. You may well want to use your sketchbook or notebook to record your ideas. A good place to start any research is the high street; it's also where you will discover how expensive commercially produced items can be. There will be no shortage of examples, from mass-produced pieces to handmade designer items. Most interior design shops will have a variety of throws and blankets on display, and I would urge you to handle these pieces, look at the combinations of fabrics used and how they are made. You will be surprised how simple some of them are. This research is not a waste of time. You will be absorbing ideas and, most important, working out what you like and don't like. Sometimes it's really easy to pin down what you do like, but much more difficult to be precise regarding your dislikes.

When you have completed your initial search, have a think about looking at some historical examples. This is where real riches lie. American quilts and coverlets are a fantastic source of ideas. When I was a student I spent a lot of time researching pioneer textiles, and I still think they are the most exquisite examples of a female-dominated art. If you are interested in an element of historical research, start in the textiles or craft section of your local library. Bookshops can be very helpful, particularly if you have specific titles in mind (see bibliography, p.94).

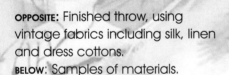

OPPOSITE: Finished throw, using vintage fabrics including silk, linen and dress cottons.
BELOW: Samples of materials.

Throws

Researching ideas

If you want to see first-rate examples of rare textiles then I would strongly recommend a visit to one of the many museums or historic houses that contain collections of domestic and fashion-related items. The Victoria and Albert Museum in London is superb, particularly the costume department, and the staff are knowledgeable and helpful. I would also sing the praises of the American Museum, located just outside Bath. It has an outstanding collection of American textiles, plus a wonderful series of room settings which date from pioneer times through to the early 20th century. It is a fascinating place to feed your imagination.

It's worth visiting historic houses to see good examples of both grand and humble textiles. You will know the ones in your area, but some of my favourites are Culzean Castle in Ayrshire, Calke Abbey in Derbyshire and Snowshill Manor in Gloucestershire. These are all National Trust properties, so are open at certain times of the year. Their collections can be accessed for private study, write in advance to the individual property to request access.

Of course, all this background information is completely optional and you may well not have the time or inclination to pursue anything more than a quick trip into your local town. What is important is that you think before you start.

Planning ahead

Making a cushion is probably more fiddly than making a throw, but working on a larger scale does present a different set of problems and rushing into the making can result in a less than satisfactory end product. Since we are also concentrating on using recycled fabrics, the task of assembling enough fabric can be daunting. As we go through the project step-by-step I'll try to give you as much information as possible regarding how to get the most out of your fabric, and what to look for when/if buying extra fabric to back your throw.

First work out the size you want your throw to be. I am making a piece that I want to drape over a small sofa, so will be working on measurements of 150 x 100cm (59 x 39½in). Decide where your throw is to be used, then work out your measurements.

Suitable fabrics

The throw I'm going to make will be 'pieced', so you won't require a single large section of fabric for the top. You will still be able to use old shirts and skirts to produce a large piece overall. However, the underside of the throw will require more fabric, so now is the time to source tablecloths, curtains, duvet covers etc. It is still possible to buy a quantity of good recycled fabric for a fraction of the price you pay for new fabric. Old domestic textiles are wonderful value and are often beautiful. For example, I have a collection of 1950s and 60s tablecloths which are immaculate but softly worn, and perfect when a large piece of fabric is required.

Just as useful are duvet covers and sheets; they often have sections of lovely detail which works brilliantly when used as backing for throws or coverlets. Curtains provide plenty of fabric, but look for softly draped material; sometimes a heavyweight upholstery fabric can make a throw feel too stiff.

Gather together your equipment for this project. You will need: your chosen fabric, tape measure and ruler, pins, sewing needles, your chosen threads and scissors.

At the end of this chapter we will work with various decorative procedures which will make your throw unique, but at this stage collect together only the items you need for the making process.

ABOVE: Fabrics I have selected to make the throw; they include an old duvet cover, a dress and a pair of curtains.

RIGHT: Materials required for this project.

Cutting and pinning

The major part of this project relies on cutting and pinning. Working on the measurements you have decided on, start cutting strips out of your material (image A). Vary the width of the strips; some narrow, maybe 6cm (2½ in), some wider, up to 20cm (8in). Don't worry if your fabric is not long enough; you can join strips together in the middle to form longer sections. Mix your fabrics, changing weight, pattern and colour. Don't be afraid to use a wide range of textures. Continue cutting strips until you have enough to form the chosen length and depth when stitched together.

Arranging the strips

Now spend some time arranging your fabric. It's useful to do this on a neutral surface, such as an old white sheet. Arrange your strips into an aesthetically pleasing composition (image B). Try not to go with your first attempt; it's worth trying different arrangements. If you want you can use your camera to record different selections. Once you are happy with the arrangement, pin your strips together using a

A Cut your strips in a variety of widths; this will give a more interesting composition to your final piece.

B Arranging the strips of fabric to work out the composition of the throw.

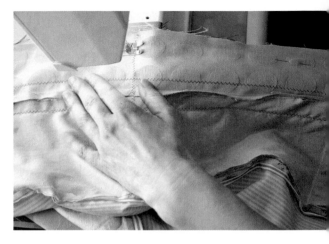

D You should start to get a feel for your throw as you stitch the strips together.

C Pinning your work together takes time, but if you stitch as you go you won't have to handle huge quantities of fabric at the same time.

E Iron all the seams flat. This creates a neater final piece.

0.5cm (¼in) seam allowance (image C). This will take some time. It's easier to work in sections, so I stitch together my strips together every time I've pinned a 25cm (10in) width. Use a medium length straight stitch and follow your pin line. The thread you use is not going to be visible so choose one that is most appropriate to your fabrics (image D).

Continue adding your strips until you have the chosen length. It's really important to press your work at this point. Turn the throw over and iron all the seams flat (image E). This will ensure a smoother finish when you put on the backing.

The backing

You now need to make a backing for the throw. You can use one whole piece of fabric if you have enough, perhaps using an old duvet cover or sheeting. However, I think it looks good if you use smaller sections of fabric; not as small as the front of the piece, but maybe dividing your backing into three sections; this will complement the striped front (image F).

To create the backing, measure your chosen fabric to match the dimensions of the front. If you are using sections of fabric, pin the pieces together, then using a medium-length straight stitch sew the fabric together until you have created your backing (image G).

If you are planning to decorate your throw with appliqué or patchwork (see p.39–41), these techniques should be completed before you stitch front and back together.

Lay out the front and back, right sides together. Pin the

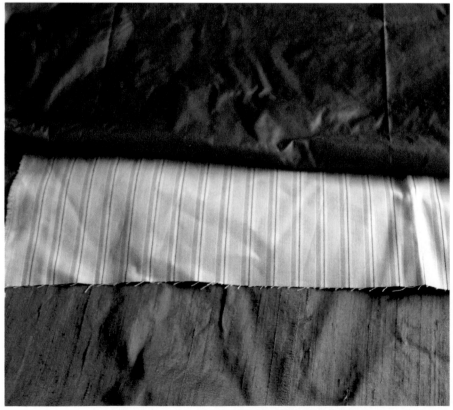

F I think the three pieces of silk and cotton I have sourced will work perfectly with the top of the throw.

G Use plenty of pins to secure the back to the top.

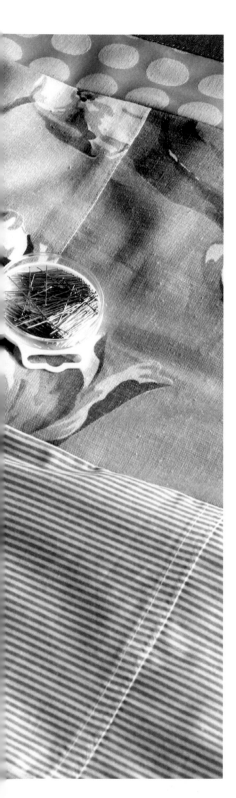

edges together, leaving a 1cm (½ in) seam allowance. You will need to put a few pins into the main body of the throw to hold it together while you are stitching the edges. Remember that you will need to turn the throw inside out after stitching, so on the final edge, finish stitching about 25cm (10in) from the end. Reverse stitch over the last 10cm (4in) of the seam to strengthen it. Turn your throw right side out, pulling it through the gap, and press the seams.

Now you need to close up the gap where you did not finish the final seam. Turn the edges of the fabric inside the throw, then pin together. As the gap left is quite small, you can sew it by hand. Use a small blanket stitch to close the gap (image H). Keep your stitches as small as possible to create a perfectly flat seam.

H Try and keep your stitches as small as possible and use a thread that matches your fabric.

Decoration

Look at your piece. Do you think it is finished? Does the top sit well on the backing fabric? If you want to, top stitch the front to the backing using some of the decorative stitches available on your machine, make sure you pin both sides together first.

Threads and stitching

This is where you can play with decorative threads, maybe trying some multi-coloured or metallic ones (image A). Don't just stitch in the same direction as your fabric strips – sew horizontally, diagonally, be imaginative. Your sewing machine, even if it is quite a basic model, should be capable of a range of stitches that can be used to produce some lovely effects.

If you don't want to work directly on your finished throw, experiment on some scraps of fabric first. Try using a different coloured thread in the bobbin – you will get flashes of that colour coming through the top stitch. The key is to keep assessing what you have done and decide when you think you have finished. You can, of course, add tassels to the cor-

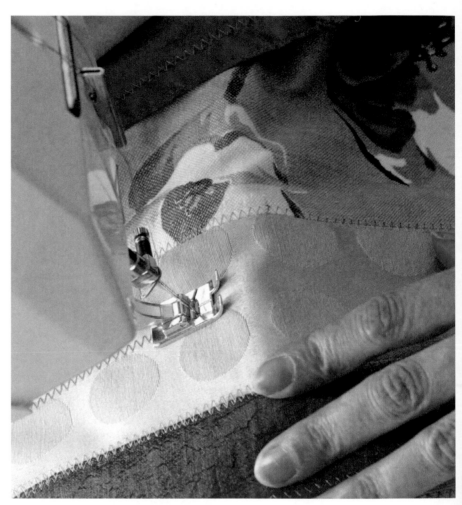

A Experiment with your machine's decorative stitches; most machines have at least five stitches that could be used decoratively. You might have to change the presser foot so consult your manual first.

ners, or trims to the edges. Think about how you decorated the cushions: you might want your throw to work with them.

Other techniques

Throws and coverlets are very simple to put together. Once you have managed to assemble enough fabric to make your item, the stitching is simplicity itself, so you can have real fun with other decoration before you finish your throw. I'm going to suggest a couple of techniques that can be employed decoratively before you stitch the top and bottom sections together.

Appliqué

When you have completed the top of your throw think about using appliqué to embellish your work. Appliqué involves cutting shapes from fabric and applying them to another fabric surface. Traditional patterns are commonly drawn from nature and include flowers and trees, as well as geometric shapes. I think it's lovely to subvert the technique and work in a more quirky way (image B).

Spread out your throw on a flat surface so that you can see the entire piece. You should have a feel already about the colours you want to work with. Search through your pile of fabrics and find some pieces that contain a bold pattern. Look for a strong floral or narrative pattern.

Once you have made your selection, isolate the part of the pattern that interests you then cut that section out (image C). Don't cut right up to the edges of the motif; leave a few millimetres around the pattern. Don't worry about fraying edges, it adds to the feel of the piece. Place the image on top of the throw. How does it look? Is it lost on a piece of work of that

B Fabrics to be used for appliqué.

C Cut out your motif but don't cut right to the edge.

scale? If so, cut out more sections of pattern and place them on the throw too. Play with overlapping the appliqué pieces, spacing them out regularly or placing them in groups. Keep standing back so you can judge your composition as a whole.

When you are happy with the arrangement, carefully pin your shapes on the throw. Thread a sharp sewing needle with a contrasting thread, using

ordinary polycotton thread. Do think about what colour you use as it will be visible. If your throw and appliqué is fairly sombre in colour, think about using a hotter, brighter contrast thread to enliven your design. Similarly, you can choose neutral-toned thread to calm down a particularly zingy bit of appliqué.

Begin handstitching your appliqué to your throw. Use small stitches to stitch over the

D Hand stitch your appliqué to the throw. Use your stitches as marks and don't worry about them all being neat and the same size.

edges of the motif, don't use a straight stitch that follows the pattern's edge (image D). Be clever with your stitch length; alternating tiny stitches with slightly longer ones. This will give a very 'hand-stitched' quality. You are using stitch as a mark-making tool and it is meant to be highly visible.

This is not the traditional way of working with appliqué, so if you do want a tight, neat quality you can use a small back stitch to attach your motifs. Continue working until you have added all your patterns. Press the material before you join the top of the throw to its backing.

Optional extra

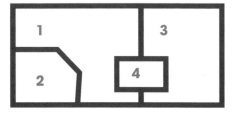

Stages

1 Cut out at least 20 circles. They don't have to be the same size.
2 Use a simple running stitch for gathering the Suffolk puffs.
3 & 4 Enjoy arranging your Suffolk puffs before you use your adhesive to fasten them to your throw.

Patchwork is another way of adding texture to a throw. Use it in sections. Again, I'm going to show you how to work in a more contemporary way, producing small areas of work and then applying them selectively to your throw.

You need to complete the throw to the stage where you are ready to join the top to the backing. As with the appliqué technique, you must spread out the throw so you can view the entire top section.

Assemble a range of small pieces of fabric, a pencil, a circle template of 3 ¾ in (9cm) diameter, scissors, sewing needle, thread and fabric adhesive.

Using your template, cut out a stack of circles from your fabrics – start with about 20 **(Stage 1)**. Again, consider your colour range. If your throw consists of plain fabrics, use patterned fabric for the patchwork. Spend some time working out your combination of colours and textures.

Thread your needle and make a simple knot at the end; you can use a matching or contrasting thread. Make a loose running stitch around the edge of the circle. Gather the circle together, knot the thread and cut **(Stage 2)**. You now have a traditional Suffolk puff.

Carry on with this technique until you have completed all the circles. You may need to make more once you have started to arrange them on your work. Start placing the Suffolk puffs on your

throw. Try grouping them together or perhaps line them up diagonally. Think about the colour and textures of the puffs – how do they work with your throw? When you are happy with the arrangement, use fabric adhesive to secure the Suffolk puffs to the throw. Do check that the glue you select is washable and is intended for craft projects **(Stage 3)**.

However you decide to decorate your throw you should have a piece of work that you can use and cherish.

4 Curtains and Blinds

OPPOSITE: The finished curtains in situ.
BELOW: The two tablecloths I am using do not match but they work well together.

AS WITH THE THROW, making curtains requires careful fabric sourcing. Depending on the size of the windows you will need quite a lot of fabric for both curtains and lining. You also need the right kind of fabric; fabric that hangs gently and isn't too stiff and bulky. Ideally the curtain fabric should be plain, such as old table linen, which tends to be cream or white. However patterned fabric can be used and hand-painting can be applied to work with the pattern. I'm not suggesting that you make heavy, interlined curtains suitable for a sitting-room. I would like to consider looser, more fluid pieces for a guest room or dining-room. The fabrics to look for are soft cottons, silks or linen. If you do find an old pair of curtains that you love then you could adapt those, and sample some of the techniques we will look at in this chapter, otherwise, to gather enough fabric you may well have to spread your net a little wider. Try visiting a flea market, car boot sale or second-hand sale. You need to be able to handle the fabric and check its condition. Old tablecloths would be ideal for this project: they provide a good quantity of fabric, they drape well and they often have fine details such as embroidery and lace edgings. The curtains described here are 'tab tops' and will therefore need a curtain pole.

In addition to the making process we are going to tackle simple hand painting on fabric.

Materials

The materials you will require are: your chosen fabric, contrasting machine thread, tape measure, scissors, artist's paintbrushes and fabric paints. Later in the chapter we will look at cutting stencils.

First decide where your curtains are going to hang. If you are feeling brave you can make full-length ones, but bear in mind the amount of fabric you are going need. I am making short curtains using two old tablecloths. Please note that my fabric, although the same colour, does not 'match'. I like this, but you might not, so choose accordingly.

For the lining you can choose a similar colour or go for something completely different, so that you see something jolly from the outside. For my lining I'm using a soft 50s cotton sheet. Please wash all your fabric before you begin, to see how much it shrinks. This is particularly important if you decide to use two different pieces of fabric.

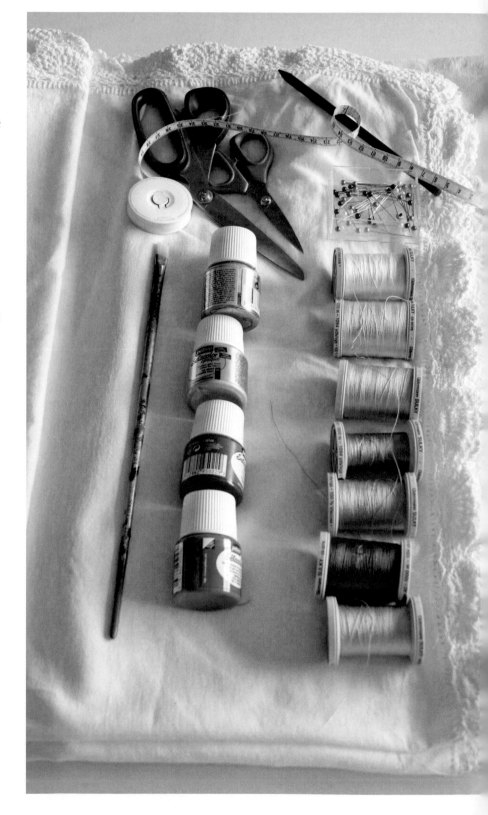

Materials required for completing this project.

A Lovely lace edges will be great for this project.

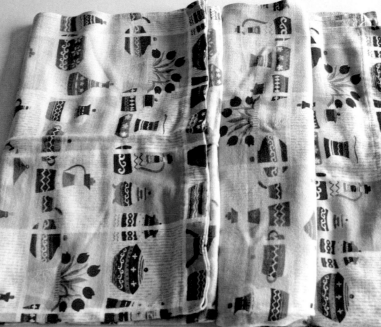

B Lining fabric. Again, you will need to have collected sufficient fabric or be prepared to join several pieces together.

Measuring up

Measure your window space. Remember you will want some fullness in your work so make sure you have plenty of fabric width, allow enough for it to gather and hang well (roughly 1½ times the width of the window). Allow for hems top and bottom and seams at the sides. If you are using tablecloths you might be able to use the fabric as it is, but if you are using other recycled fabric you will need to cut it to size. Try to use any existing hems; it will make your stitching time shorter, plus you often get lovely details at the edges of vintage fabric (image A).

You will also need to cut out the lining. The lining will be inserted underneath the tabs on the back of the curtains, so it is shorter than the curtain itself. The tabs I am making are 15cm (6in) in length and 17cm (6¾ in) wide, so that means my lining will be 15cm (6in) shorter than the curtain.

Select a fabric for the tabs that is either the same or similar to the lining (image B). When measuring for your tabs, bear in mind that the curtain and lining will need to move freely across the curtain pole. If your tabs are too small the fabric will not draw smoothly.

NB: The curtain is decorated before the lining and tabs are added. For making instructions for the lining and tabs see p.50–51.

Decoration

Once you have your pieces cut you need to move to a large enough surface to spread out the fabric. You will be using fabric paint, so make sure the surface isn't precious. Spread an old sheet underneath the fabric if you are concerned (image A). For the time being you will only be working on the front of the curtain, so put the lining on one side.

At this stage you are going to produce a simple surface pattern using fabric paint. For inspiration consult books, look through magazines, and take photographs. Try and record some ideas in your sketch-book. For this project I have been looking at a couple of books I have about Parisian pâtisseries. I love the colours, shapes and decoration involved in both the buildings and the products they sell (image B). I usually spend some time drawing and making notes and considering how to simplify what I am looking at. Even if you aren't confident about drawing you will still absorb information from your research. You can always use tracing paper to trace imagery that you like, then use that to work with.

A Protect your table from the fabric paints.

B My inspiration for these patterns came from this lovely book about those famous French macaroons – Ladurée.

C If you are feeling confident, draw freehand direct onto the cloth, otherwise you can use tracing paper to transfer your imagery.

Once you have decided what pattern you want to use, you must transfer that image to your fabric. I use a standard HB pencil to draw directly onto my fabric. From the simplified image of extravagant Parisian cakes I have drawn my image along the bottom edge of the fabric. Don't feel your two sides have to match. Maybe one section could have more imagery than the other, or perhaps you would prefer the image to travel up the closing edges of the curtains. I draw freehand, but you can trace your design and transfer that onto your fabric (image C).

Fabric paint

You will need fabric paint for this project. I use a water-based paint, which is non-toxic and very easy to use, that I buy from the local art shop. There are a variety of brands, but for this project you need a paint suitable for medium-weight fabrics. These have a thicker texture than a paint for use on silk. If your art shop is good there will be a wide range of colours, including metallics and pearlescent hues. Don't forget basic colour theory: mix red and blue to

make purple, yellow and blue to make green, red and yellow to make orange, and black and white to make grey, so buy basic colours that you can then mix into more unusual combinations. As fabric paint is easy to mix, try mixing different tones, or add a metallic paint to achieve a subtle glow.

All these trials could be recorded on a spare piece of medium-weight calico – write next to the swatch of colour what colours you mixed to achieve that particular tone. Try and gauge the quantities of paint you will need for a particular area of design. If you are mixing colours, be careful you don't run out of a particular colour before you have finished a selected area. By the same token, don't mix too much, as it's a shame to waste your paints (image D, p.48).

Brushes

You will need an artist's paintbrush to apply the paint. Choose an appropriate size depending on how big an area you need to colour. I always prefer a blunt-edged brush as I can achieve a sharp line and perfect edge, but if you are painting fine lines of colour you may want a more delicate point. You don't have to spend a fortune on a beautiful brush: you need something practical and robust that won't shed hairs and will stand up to the rigours of cleaning.

If you enjoy using fabric paint, start to collect brushes of different sizes and shapes and, perhaps, some mini-rollers for applying colour to larger areas. You can also use small decorator's brushes, which are sometimes cheaper and definitely tougher.

Applying the paint

Now all the preparatory work is complete, the fun can begin!

Make sure your fabric is as flat as possible, though it really doesn't need to be stretched. Do make sure you have some paper or old fabric underneath your curtain, otherwise any paint that bleeds through the fabric will stain the surface you are working on.

Start to paint. There are no hard and fast rules; you may well want certain areas of image to be painted quite thickly, and some to be lighter and more delicate. As you are using a water-based medium, you can add water to the paint to create more of a soft stain.

Try to complete all the painting in one session, especially if you have mixed your colours. The paints I use are quite thick, so it's easy to paint right up to the edges of an already painted area without getting any bleeding of colours. If you are using more watery colours then allow one to settle before adding another colour in close proximity to the first. Obviously, if you paint wet colour directly on top of wet colour, the two will merge.

Leave the paint to dry for at least an hour. You must then iron your work on the reverse side. Set your iron according to the fabric you are using and make sure you iron the back of the image thoroughly, as this fixes the colour.

D A selection of the fabric paints I'm going to use.

Fabric pens

This can be the starting point for more embellishment if you like. In addition to fabric paint you can also use fabric pens, which look exactly like a marker pen, but are dye-based rather than ink-filled. These pens are ideal for adding linear interest to your work. You could outline your imagery, work on top of the pattern or add text. If you do use fabric pens, make sure you iron the back of the work again to fix the new marks.

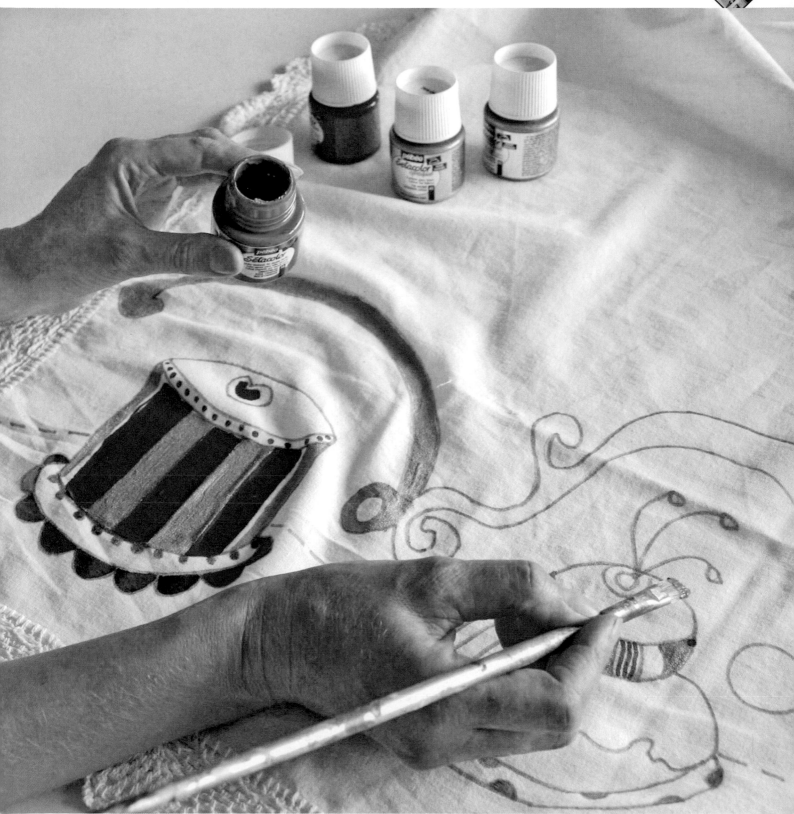

E Paint as carefully and quickly as you can. If you have mixed your colours ensure you have enough for the areas you are tackling, and as they dry quite fast try to use them up before they become difficult to work with.

Finishing and lining the curtains

Unless you are using old tablecloths, as I am, you will first have to sew the side seams of your curtains and make a hem top and bottom. You will then be ready to make the tabs which will support the curtains.

Tabs

Depending on how wide your curtains are, you need to work out how many tabs you are going to need. Tabs should be spaced 5–10cm (2–4in) apart. My fabric is quite lightweight and doesn't need lots of closely spaced tabs to support it. If heavier fabric is used more tabs will be required to support the weight. If the tabs are too close together it will make the curtains more difficult to open and close. When you cut out your tabs, make sure you add 2.5cm (1in) to each side to allow for the seam. Stitch a hem on each side of your tab (image A). As stated earlier my tabs are 15cm (6in) long and 17cm (6¾in) wide. Each curtain is 125cm (49in) wide, so I am going to make 6 tabs per curtain which the curtain pole will slide through.

Assemble your tabs then pin them to the top of your curtains

A Tabs need to be the same size and have a seam allowance.

B Pin your tabs to the curtains so that you can achieve an equal distance between each tab.

on the reverse side (image B). Using a medium-length straight stitch sew your tabs to your curtains top and bottom, removing the pins as you go.

Lining

When you have finished the tab stitching you should have a pair of curtains, albeit unlined. Measure your curtains from underneath your tabs and allow 5cm (2in) for a hem at the bottom. Add 2cm (1in) seam allowance at each side and at the top, this is because you are going to hem the sides where the lining is attached. Pin your hems, then using a medium-length straight stitch sew the sides and bottom hems following your

pin lines. When your hems are complete, pin the top edge of the lining to the curtain, directly under the tabs. Make sure you pin your lining with the hems on the reverse side (image C). Stitch the lining to the curtain along its top edge. I quite like to secure the lining to the curtain at the top only, allowing the lining to float free. If you want to, you can stitch the sides together to create a more orthodox arrangement.

Your curtains are now complete and ready to hang on the pole. If, at a later date, you need to wash the curtains, try hand-washing them then spinning on a gentle cycle. Any item you make from recycled fabrics has to be treated sensitively when it comes to cleaning.

C Lots of pinning is required at this stage to make sure your lining fits correctly.

Roller blind

If you have produced a successful set of curtains, perhaps you would like to try making a printed roller blind. It's not complicated, as you can buy roller blind kits (image A), which provide you with all the essentials and allow you to choose your own fabric. I am going to assume that you have bought a kit. Select a piece of fabric that is sufficient for your space. It can be plain or patterned, and if it's plain it's easier to use bolder painting. You might want to make a blind that works with the curtains you have made, maybe to fit the same window, particularly if the curtains are made from very lightweight fabric.

A Roller blind kit. Don't attempt to make your own from scratch at this stage.

Stencils

At this stage I'm going to suggest you get to grips with using stencils to create imagery for your blind. You will require heavyweight paper, a craft knife and pencil, artists brushes, fabric paints and embellishments such as beads and sequins (image B). If the blind is going to work with the curtains then you might want to replicate some of the imagery you used on them,

but if the blind is to stand alone then you need some new ideas. Source images that appeal to you, then to make things simple, photocopy that imagery, playing around with scale if you want to. When you have an image you are satisfied with use your craft knife to cut out the selected shape. What is left after the shape has been removed is your stencil (image C).

Using your stencil, trace the shape onto the blind. Think where you want to place the imagery. Mine is at the bottom of the blind so that you see the imagery when the blind is not pulled down. You might want to place your stencils along the side of the blind or down the middle. Using your fabric paints work into the shapes you have made (image D). Leave your painted pattern to dry.

B Materials required for doing simple stencilling.

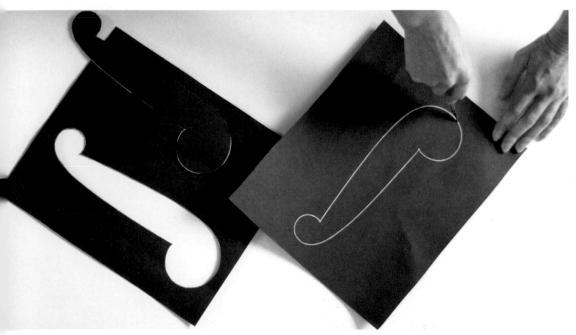

C Cutting out your stencil. Remember you will use the negative shape as your stencil.

D Painting into the stencilled shapes.

Iron the dried fabric on its reverse to set the colours. Follow the instructions supplied with your roller blind to produce the finished item.Look carefully at what you have produced. If you want to, you can add more embellishment to your curtains and blind. Think about some of the appliqué techniques practised in earlier chapters. Maybe put a row of Suffolk puffs on the closing edges of your curtains or add a beautiful tassel to pull the blind down. Have fun!

E Finished blind.

5 Table Linen

We are going back to basics with this chapter in terms of the making process, but I think what we are going to make will form a perfect blank canvas for decoration, both machine stitched and using beads, buttons and sequins. By their very nature the pieces in this chapter are smaller scale, which is less daunting when considering decoration. You can also use pre-existing pieces, giving them a makeover using print and stitch. I thought it would be nice to produce a table runner too, which can be left on a table for decorative purposes.

I'm using plain fabric for the table linen, but some patterning would be great as the machine stitching could emphasise some of the pattern. Practically speaking, you need to appreciate that table linen will get grubby more frequently, so you have to ensure that any fabric paint, print or embellishment is washable. And if you are going to make the items from scratch, please wash the fabric first.

ABOVE: Assorted fabric to be used for the table linen.
OPPOSITE: Table runner and embroidered napkins.

Table Linen

Materials

The materials you will need for these pieces are: pre-existing table linen or sufficient fabric to make a tablecloth and four napkins, sewing machine, machine embroidery threads, general purpose machine thread, Nymo thread, fabric paint, a selection of old buttons, small beads, sequins, scissors, an embroidery hoop and the embroidery foot for your machine.

You should find it very easy to track down old linen. A trawl of several charity shops netted me several tablecloths, a stash of pretty lace-edged napkins and some fantastic crocheted doilies. None of these items cost more than £1, all are clean and in good order and most have beautiful decorative edges. If you are going to re-vamp existing linen try to buy neutral-coloured pieces, which will work more successfully with the decoration you are going to try.

If you can't find any existing pieces you will need to find sufficient quantity of fabric to make a tablecloth, though you don't have to use the same fabric to make the napkins and runner. I think

Materials required for this project.

Existing table linen. I have washed and ironed all these pieces.

it's more interesting to have a mismatched quality to the work you make. Try to find

some pristine sheets or mid-weight curtains which will give enough fabric for your needs.

Making instructions

Before we start embellishing, let's just deal with some simple making instructions to enable you to make the items from scratch. If you are creating the items from anything other than table linen you must wash and iron the fabric first. Once you have checked that your fabric is washable, measure the table and then cut your fabric accordingly. Allow for an overhang on all sides, plus ¾ in (2cm) all round for a hem allowance.

Set your sewing machine to a small zig-zag stitch and don't feel you have to use threads that match your cloth. You could also have a different coloured thread in the bobbin to the one you are sewing with. Pin the fabric so that you have an even hem all the way around the cloth (image A). Zig-zag stitch over the hem edge, removing the pins as you go. Follow the same instructions to make the napkins. Do be generous with the size of the napkins – large ones look so much better. Iron everything flat, concentrating on the edges. You should now have a functioning tablecloth and napkins (image B).

A Hem your fabric on all sides.

B Once you have hemmed all the pieces you should have a functioning set of table linen.

Table runner

To make the table runner select a piece of fabric that you are happy to have on the table when it is not being used. Consider the length; it can be long enough to drape over the ends of the table, or just long enough to sit on top, while the width can be as narrow as you feel is aesthetically pleasing. Remember, you don't have to make a runner for your dining table. You could choose a smaller, occasional table or side table. This will enable you to source smaller quantities of fabric.

Cut your fabric to the desired length and width and make a hem in the same way as with the tablecloth. If you are using a lightweight fabric you can back the runner with a more substantial piece of fabric. I recently sourced a gorgeous section of roller towel linen; it has a lovely weight and beautiful wavy edges. It was not particularly cheap, but it would be perfect for this type of project. If you do need to back your work cut a piece of fabric the same size as your top, hem in the same way then sew the two pieces together using straight stitch.

The runner I have made for this project is an elongated rectangle, but feel free to be creative with the narrow ends of the piece. You could make the ends pointed, curved or scalloped. Mine is rectangular as it is to have tassels at the corners.

If you are using existing, reclaimed textiles all you need to do is ensure that the fabric is ironed and clean.

Machine embroidery

We can't delay any longer – you are now going to have a crack at machine embroidery. It's easier if you begin with the napkins; they are smaller and infinitely more controllable. I'm going to work with a very simple floral motif with trailing leaves. These are not botanically accurate by any means. I want the imagery to be loose and flowing, changing colour as I work across the fabric. Don't be tempted to work all over the piece. Machine embroidery is quite dense and will cause the fabric to contract. If you work too heavily you will find that the overall piece distorts.

Embroidery hoops

Traditionally these are two wooden hoops, the outer ring being the larger and having a screw to tighten. Hoops are very useful to prevent distortion and can be used for both machine and hand embroidery. I would suggest you use a hoop for this project (these can be bought from suppliers, see p.94) . Take your fabric and place the smaller of the two rings under your napkin, making sure you have spare material around the edge of the hoop. Put the bigger of the hoops over the top and push down firmly; this will stretch your fabric. Tighten the screw on the outer ring. The fabric should be really taut (image C).

If you want to draw a design

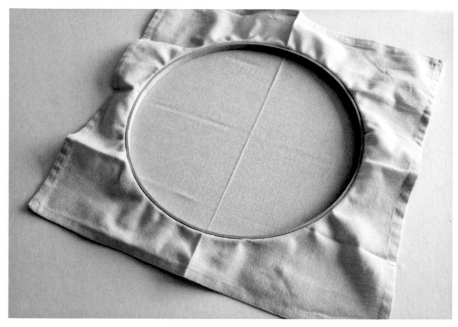

C Stretch your fabric as taut as possible. If the fabric is too baggy it will distort as you stitch.

on your napkin before you stitch, use a pencil to create a delicate outline. Don't use anything too hard or dark as this will show through the stitching.

Before you begin stitching you will need to consult your sewing machine manual and follow the instructions to allow your machine to work in embroidery mode. My Bernina is fairly standard in that I drop the feed dog, change the foot and adjust the tension slightly. Your machine will differ slightly, but it is a simple operation. When you machine embroider, you don't want the feed dog pulling the fabric through the machine, so when you drop the feeder you control where the fabric goes (image D).

Think about the colour of thread you want to use. If you put a separate colour in the

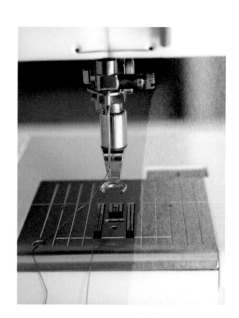

D My embroidery foot for the Bernina 1008, with the feed dog below it.

bobbin, the bobbin colour will show slightly as you stitch on to the fabric.

Take the napkin you have stretched using the hoop and position the machine needle above the area you are beginning with. Drop the presser foot lever and, using the handwheel, lower the needle through the fabric and bring it back up. Repeat this action.

Now, using your foot pedal, begin to stitch. At first it will feel a little odd – as the feed dog is down you will be responsible for moving the fabric around. The trick is to start slowly, and move the hoop carefully. If this is your first attempt at using free machining it would be a good idea to practise first on a spare piece of fabric.

Work into your design by moving the hoop with small fluid movements. Feel free to change your colours as you complete different sections. Try and really build up certain areas, stitching heavily into the design, other parts of the work can be delicately delineated (image E, p.62). Try using a metallic thread to highlight specific sections. Vary your stitch length by moving the hoop with larger movements. If all this feels like patting your head and rubbing your tummy at the same time,

E I am using quite dense stitching in some areas and looser, trailing stitches in others.

all I can say is that you have to practise and be patient. Try not to get cross with your machine – it's not its fault! You may well have to adjust your tension, particularly when using metallic threads.

Assess your work as you go, and don't be afraid to play with colour. You will have to adjust the position of the fabric in the embroidery hoop as you progress. I have worked along the edges of my napkin, as I have a lovely lace corner

which I am going to work into and embellish at a later stage (image F). If you are making a set of napkins don't think they all have to be exactly the same. It's a good idea to either make or source fabric that is a similar size but not necessarily a perfect match. None of the pieces I am working on come from the same family, but all work really well together. The embroidery and decoration won't be perfectly repeatable, so enjoy the one-off quality you produce.

F Existing lace edges on the napkin

Sequins, buttons and beads

Once you are satisfied with the embroidery you have created, iron the fabric and get busy with sequins, buttons and beads (image G). When applying such surface decoration you will need to use a stronger thread to secure it. I use Nymo, which you can purchase from craft shops or on the internet. Nymo is available in a variety of colours, comes on small spools which cost approximately £1, and is very tough. It's great for simple beading and knots securely when you have finished the decoration. You can use a heavier weight of sewing thread, but as discussed previously these items obviously need to be washed frequently, and you don't want all your beads falling off after one wash. Nymo thread is certainly stronger.

Beads

A note on the beads, sequins and buttons I use. I use Guttermann beads size 9; these have a sufficiently large central hole to allow a small hand-sewing needle to pass through. Smaller beads are available, but you will need to buy specific beading needles to apply those. Beading needles are incredibly fine, and usually include a threading device which stops you from screaming in frustration. There are many shops and internet sites selling beads and related products (see p.94 for stockists).

Sequins

Sequins are fantastic to use with interiors projects. I love the big 2.5cm (1in) sequins which have their threading hole at the top. I like to layer them almost like scales on a fish and they also look wonderful strung densely on edges of fabric. The 0.5cm (¼in) sequins with a centre threading hole are also great for lines of decoration. I buy a lot of my trimmings from an online haberdashery store called Josyrose which has a wide range of decorations in a myriad of different colours. Buy a few small packs of different

G Equipment for embellishing.

H Tiny scraps of fabric can be used when making self-cover buttons.

shapes and sizes of sequins and have a play with how you use them. Try stringing them with different coloured threads, add them thickly in small areas, and use them to outline particular sections of pattern. You can't really make a mistake and it's easy to remove them if they don't work.

Buttons

I enjoy a very peculiar relationship with buttons and veer on the edge of having a button phobia. However, I do love carefully selected cards of vintage buttons and spend a small fortune on them. I urge you to start collecting buttons. Most old garments you acquire will have buttons or other fastenings; cut them off, store them in jars and use them decoratively. They look lovely stitched in groups, using different colours and textures, and, bearing in mind this is a book about reviving old textiles, they represent a spirit of thrift.

You can also make your own, using self-cover button kits. These are readily available from markets and haberdashery stores. They consist of an upper piece which you stretch your fabric over, securing it with the lower piece which holds the fabric in place. You can make some lovely fastenings for your projects using these, plus they look wonderful as decoration (image H).

Decorating the napkins

Work into the machine embroidery with your chosen beads and decoration. Follow certain parts of your design with the beads, and then allow your decoration to trail across other sections of the surface. If you have any existing crochet or lace on your napkins try emphasising areas with a few small beads or flat sequins. Again, change the decoration on each napkin you make (image J).

Decorating the tablecloth

When you are ready to work on the tablecloth, remember the scale is completely different, and if you work with small-scale decoration it will take a long time to complete. So consider using fabric paints on the tablecloth. I am using simple circles which I will then decorate and stitch into.

Spread out your tablecloth on a large, clean surface and either use a compass or draw around a plate or glass to create your circles (image I).

When you are happy with your design, begin painting (image K). Consider the colours you used when you decorated the napkins, and select fabric paints which you feel work well with those. Complete the

I Draw a range of simple shapes on the tablecloth.

J This is the time when you can sit and really play with your surface decoration. Remember to vary the scale of your decoration and the textures of different items; and have fun with colour.

65

K Paint directly onto the tablecloth.

L Emphasise some of your print with machine embroidery.

painting and leave your work to dry thoroughly. Iron the back of the cloth to fix the colour.

Now, using your sewing machine and an embroidery hoop, work with free embroidery stitch into the design you have painted. Try experimenting with some text; stitch words or sentences across the tablecloth surface. If you don't feel confident, use a pencil to create the text before sewing (image J). You might find you need a larger embroidery hoop because of the increase in scale, but feel free to dispense with the hoop altogether, so that the embroidery flows freely. It

will feel odd not to have the support of the hoop, but I hardly ever use one now as I like the freedom to stitch where I want. If you are going hoop-less remember you will have to really control the fabric, and endeavour to keep the area you are stitching as taut as possible.

What you want to achieve is a set of table linen that is in harmony, not one that replicates itself. You should now be able to embrace the unique!

Decorating the table runner

The final strand in this chapter is to continue your newly honed

decorative skills and work on the table runner. I like the idea of runners as they provide instant decoration in a room. They also provide a perfect cover for an imperfect piece of furniture. The idea is that you leave the runner in place, so consider what other colours and textures you have in your room. This piece does not have to work with the table linen you have just produced, but if you particularly liked a certain area of decoration then feel free to continue with the theme.

You can, of course, use any existing table linen you might have. This type of project is perfect for using scraps of

M Echo some of the imagery from the tablecloth on the table runner. Here the use of circles is continued as a theme.

decorative trims that I am sure you are now assiduously squirrelling away. Again, the runner is larger and any decoration needs to work with the increased scale. But you don't have to automatically scale up the embellishment; sometimes areas of small but intense decoration can be lovely on a bigger object.

I am using the fabric paints to produce a design that works on the top edge of the runner. Using the same template as you did for the tablecloth, draw a series of circles on the runner. Paint the circles with your fabric paints and leave to dry thoroughly (image M). Iron the reverse of the runner to fix the colour. Again, use your sewing machine and work with free embroidery on top of the print

Stitched and painted tablecloth with embroidered napkins.

Table runner with embroidered napkins.

you have created. After the tablecloth and napkins you have produced, you should have more of a definite idea about the type of embroidery you want to use on the runner. Think about beginning the stitch at one end of the runner and trailing it over the print. You don't have to embroider over the entire piece; select areas that you want to be focal points.

When you have finished the stitching, select any decorations you want to use and add them to your mix. I am using large sequins on one end and rows of smaller sequins on the other (image N). A final flourish is a couple of large, ready-made tassels (which can be relatively cheap to buy) that you can add beads and sequins to; this makes a mass-produced trim unique. Simply take your tassels and add your selected beads around the centre. There isn't a right and wrong way with this, so go your own way and add ribbon, buttons and whatever works for you (image O).

After all your hard work lay the table and invite some friends over for afternoon tea and cakes.

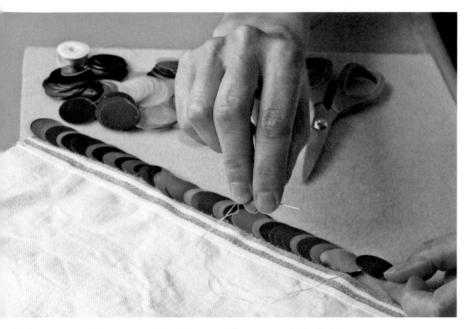

N Large sequins are perfect for creating a really lush trim.

O Embellish your ready-made tassels to make them unique.

6 Furniture

ABOVE: Detail of footstool in progress.
OPPOSITE: Finished footstool.

F IRST – I AM NOT an upholsterer and this chapter is not about traditional upholstery methods; it's about re-modelling what you already have and enjoying your revived pieces. You won't need any specialist skills, just a bit of time and some space to spread your work out. As you are going to be using reclaimed fabric, you will also need a reasonable amount of fabric. This shouldn't be too much of a problem as, in some cases, you can re-work your existing fabric. However, if you are working on an item that has fixed covers you will need sufficient fabric to re-cover. I have left existing covers on all the furniture I've salvaged, heaven alone knows what's underneath some stuff, so I use what's available as a firm base. Later in the chapter we will discuss buying old furniture at auction, stripping it and re-working the existing covers, using them as templates or bases.

Choosing a piece

To start with you have to make a few decisions about the piece you are going to tackle. I wouldn't suggest that you start with a large sofa! Look at your furniture and assess which pieces could be likely candidates. If possible, you want something with a square, chunky shape, without too many curves and indents. A small armchair or footstool would be ideal.

Don't be tempted to be too ambitious, or choose a piece that is really precious. You want something that will help you learn. If you pick an item that is in constant use you might have to restrict the amount of decoration you can add; children in particular enjoy playing with decoration, not always to its advantage!

It's going to be difficult to supply you with exact patterns and dimensions for this project as you won't be tackling the same piece of furniture that I have. However, the principles are the same whatever you make.

Your material list includes: selected item of furniture, range of larger-size pieces of

Materials required for this project.

reclaimed fabric, machine sewing threads, pins, tracing paper, ruler, tape measure, scissors and a selection of decorative items. Depending on the piece of furniture you might also need upholstery tacks, a small hammer and upholstery needles.

Footstool

I am going to work with an old velvet footstool which I love, as does my dog, so I need to use a fairly robust fabric and consider carefully some dog-proof embellishment (image A). The velvet that is currently in place has faded and looks slightly spotted, but I don't want to dispose of it. I'll have it cleaned and alternate it with the new cover.

If your chosen piece has a similar loose cover you can do the same, or leave the cover in place and use it as an extra lining for the fabric you now intend to use. Another idea to consider is to re-vamp the covers that are currently doing the job; you might find this a gentler introduction to working with larger three-dimensional pieces.

My first step will be to thoroughly clean my item. The cushion on the footstool is removable from the base and underneath the velvet cover is a calico cushion cover. This will be left in place. Check what your furniture is made of, and what type of stuffing is being used in the cushion pads. Is the frame in good condition? The footstool has solid wood legs, a woven base and a

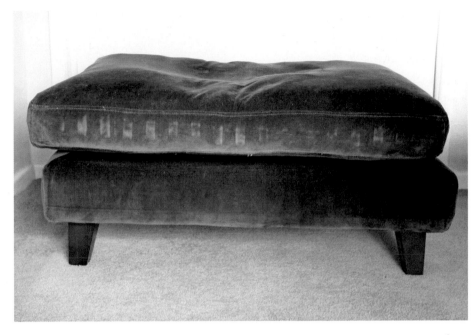

A My much-loved velvet footstool.

feather-stuffed top cushion. The general condition of the piece is good (image B).

Don't feel that you have to use the same fabric over the whole piece of furniture. It's unlikely that you will be able to find enough fabric from reclaimed sources to re-cover an entire chair, for example.

I think the piece will look much more contemporary if you use a variety of fabrics, including different weights, colours and textures. I have made a selection that includes old furnishing fabric, a linen tablecloth and some heavier weight dress fabric;

B I need to check that the piece is in generally good condition.

the fabrics are both plain and patterned (image C). I want the end product to look completely different to its former incarnation.

Making a pattern

It's essential that you cut a pattern for the new furniture covers. You can use pattern paper which has a grid printed on it – this will help to make your pattern more accurate. You will find pattern paper in your local haberdashery shop. I am using tracing paper as I find it easier to make a larger-scale pattern with it.

Measure your furniture's different components: back, arms, seat etc. Take as many measurements as you can and record them carefully (image D). This is particularly important if you are recovering a more complicated structure. Once you have made your measurements draw out your basic shapes. You will need separate pieces for any removable sections. Remember to add a hem allowance to all your pattern pieces if they need to be joined together.

The footstool needs a pattern for the cushion and one for the base. The pattern for the cushion seat consists of four pieces; the base only needs one piece. The fastening for the seat cover will be overlapped fabric, similar to the cushion cover we made earlier. I think this gives a neat finish.

C A variety of fabrics are going to be used for this project; I want it to have a lovely patched and pieced quality.

D Take plenty of measurements before cutting your paper pattern.

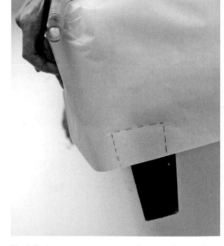

E Make sure your pattern allows for the legs. A separate pattern is required for the base.

The base is slightly more complicated in that I have to allow for the legs (image E), so I have cut the pattern with deep 'U' shapes which will be cut out, hemmed and then folded around the legs. I am going to secure the base fabric with upholstery tacks.

Starting with the base pattern I am going to cut out the fabric. I am using a lovely 1950s curtain fabric. It's a medium weight and I really like the pattern and colour. Obviously, the cushion seat will cover a good portion of the base fabric, so if you are tackling a similar project, feel free to use a more neutral, less special fabric for the areas that aren't visible. Check that your fabric fits the designated area. Pin the hems then, using a medium-length straight stitch, sew the hems, removing the pins as you go (image F). Iron your fabric and check again that the fabric fits as it should.

For the seat cushion I have four pattern pieces: one piece for the top, one long piece for

G My pattern has four pieces and plenty of colour variation.

F Create the corners for the base material. Pin your hems before you stitch the base fabric.

the sides and two for the bottom. I am going to use fabrics in a variety of different patterns and colours as I want the seat to have an eclectic quality (image G). Once the pattern pieces are cut I am going to sew the sides to the top, wrong sides together. The underside of the seat cushion is made from two separate pieces of material, with a hem at each

side of the opening edges. The opening for the cushion on the footstool works on the same principle as the opening for the cushion in chapter two (allow the edges to overlap in order to get the cushion in). Sew the underside fabric to the side fabric. The corners of the new cushion cover are bulky and need to be fed slowly through the sewing machine. The stitched edges will need to be trimmed of excess fabric before the new cover is turned right side out. At this point it's important to check that the piece fits the cushion seat pad (image H). Iron the new cover thoroughly, pressing the seams flat. To fix the base cover to the footstool frame I am going to place the new cover over the base, pull it taut and secure with pins. I then

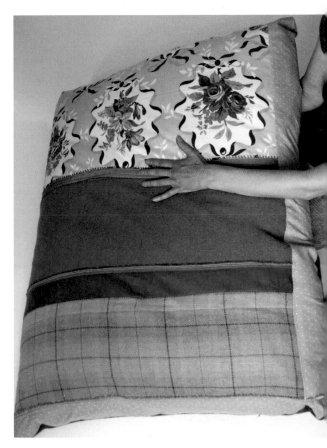

H Stitch all your pieces together, then check that the cover fits the pad. The fabric on the reverse side of the pad should overlap generously.

Furniture

turn the base over. Beginning with a longer side the new fabric is secured with upholstery tacks: small, flat-headed, sharp tacks that are easy to knock into wood (image I). If you don't want to use tacks, try using Velcro to secure your new covers, which makes removal for cleaning much easier.

Trimmings

I now have a new footstool, but feel it's not quite finished. I am going to show you how to make your own upholstery trimmings. I love decoration on individual pieces of furniture but don't like the prices charged for often quite simple trims.

Pattern and layout for the footstool (not to scale)

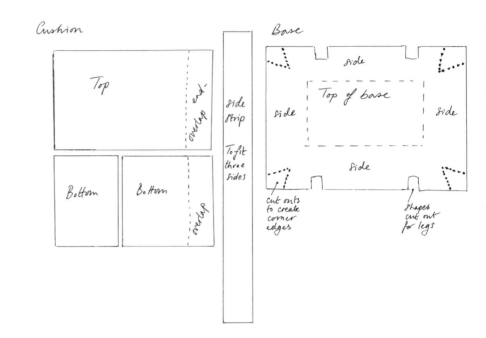

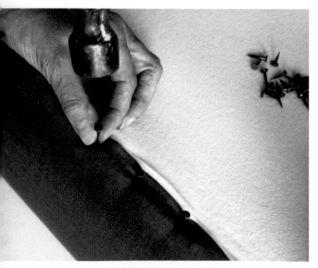

I   Upholstery tacks are small and very sharp, and they are easy to hammer into your furniture.

J   Existing trim and a selection of ribbons that I have collected over a period of time. These will be perfect for remaking into new trim.

When you are sourcing fabric for these projects keep your eyes open for bags of old braid, which can look very old-fashioned, but can be transformed into something quite spectacular. Any pieces of ribbon that you may have or can collect would also be useful (image J). I am making trim to go around the top edge of the new footstool seat cushion.

Take a length of existing trim and a corresponding length of wide ribbon and also one of narrow ribbon. Place the trim in the middle of the wide ribbon and, using a machine embroidery thread of a contrasting colour, stitch the trim to the ribbon. You can use whatever stitch you like; try experimenting with one of the decorative stitches on your machine. Once the trim is secure, place the narrow ribbon above the trim and sew that to the wider ribbon (image K). Select further decoration such as sequins or beads and apply those to your new trimming. I get carried away when making new embellishments and for the footstool the revamped trim will alter subtly on each edge. I will keep the width consistent but vary the backing ribbon. In addition the beads and sequins will alter as I progress.

When you are happy with your trimming, hand stitch it on to the new cover. I use Nymo thread for this as it is a stronger thread and more suitable for upholstery work (image L). Alternatively, you can use fabric adhesive. You can continue to experiment with trims, adding different ribbons, pompoms, scraps of silk and buttons. You could even make small quantities and save them for future projects.

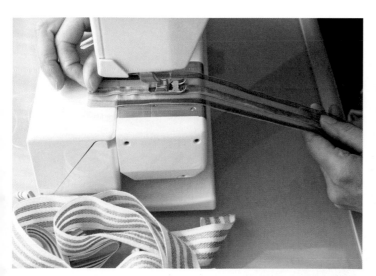

K Enjoy trying different combinations of ribbon and trim stitched together.

L Hand stitch your trim onto your piece. You can use fabric adhesive if you find the stitching hard going.

Auction house bargains

I am now going to suggest you try working with a piece of furniture that you find at an auction house or junk shop. When I talk about furniture picked up at auction, I'm not talking antiques. Consult your telephone directory to find a saleroom in a small town rather than one in a big city, which can be a lot pricier. Most sales have preview days, and it's worth having a browse and looking closely at any pieces that catch your eye. Check for basic soundness: is it fit for purpose, is it riddled with woodworm, is it more trouble than it's worth?

I have found a wooden-framed chair with a back and seat that need replacing. The chair is a lovely shape and will work well with my other furniture. It's not an old piece, cost just £8, and as it only needs stripping and small areas of fabric replacing it's perfect in terms of time. Obviously, if you are feeling brave and have the time you might well want to try something more ambitious. If you decide to use a chair, try to find a chair with a removable seat.

My auction house bargain.

Stripping and cleaning

Before I strip and clean the chair I'm going to remove the pieces of fabric so I can use them as patterns. The chair has been coated with a thick, dark varnish and is generally a bit grubby. I'm using a product called Nitromors which is a powerful paint stripper. If you are going to use a substance such as this you need to work outside or with very good ventilation (image A). Wear a mask and rubber gloves, keep it away from pets and children and try not to splash it on your skin. Just follow the instructions and you'll be fine.

I'm going to wax my chair once I've finished removing the old varnish; this will bring out the grain and protect the wood. You can also limewax your piece; this will stain your furniture slightly and give it a chalky appearance (image B). Limewax can be purchased from most good DIY stores or picture framers.

A Paint stripper needs to be used with caution (use outdoors if possible).

B Limewaxing gives old furniture a lovely soft quality and emphasises the grain of the wood.

Furniture

Upholstery

Try to use the existing upholstery as patterns for your new cover. Think about the type of fabric you are going to choose. I want this chair to be functional rather than merely decorative, so delicate fabrics won't work. As the areas to be recovered aren't huge I'm going to treat myself and buy some fabric. This is cheating, I know, but the website I'm going to use to source my fabric specialises in reclaimed fabrics. Its run by a lady called Donna Flower who is incredibly knowledgeable, her website is a pleasure to use and she is constantly adding new fabrics (see stockists, p.94). As I only need a metre (yard) of fabric and the chair was so cheap I think I can justify this little diversion (image C).

Patterns

Using tracing paper or pattern paper make yourself a pattern in the same way as when re-upholstering your earlier piece (see p.74). Cut out your shapes from your selected fabric (image D). I need to ensure that I cut sufficient material to allow me to pull it taut over the chair frame, but I don't need to hem the fabric because any uneven edges will be hidden by the trim.

C A collection of beautiful old fabrics that I have sourced from Donna Flower.

D Cut a paper pattern to fit your piece of furniture.

My next step is to replace the seat cover and back of my chair. Starting with the chair back I am going to secure the fabric with upholstery tacks. As the tacks are visible I'm going to create a trim to cover this edge.

Trim

Taking a bundle of ribbon, I'm going to join a variety of lengths and widths to make enough to fit around the fabric on the back.

When you have the desired length of trim, set your sewing machine to embroidery mode. Using contrasting machine embroidery thread, stitch a trailing motif along the length of your ribbon. Don't feel you have to use an embroidery hoop for this; any distortion created through stitching will add rather than detract from your final trim (image E). Using a good quality textile or craft adhesive, stick your finished trim in place. Allow the glue to dry thoroughly.

E Don't worry about any distortion created when stitching; you want your braid to have a wavy quality.

F A staple gun is often easier to use when you want to secure fabric to a section of furniture. This is strong enough to fix it permanently.

Fitting the seat cover requires the fabric to be stretched tightly across the pad making certain that the corners are neat. If the seat is removeable, then take it out first. Pin the fabric in place as you work before tacking the fabric in place on the underside. The new seat can now be replaced. If you want to you can use a staple gun to secure the new fabric to the base. It's sometimes easier to get a tighter, more professional finish if you staple rather than tack (image F). You should now have a unique piece of furniture which is both useful and lovely.

7 A Special Project

ABOVE: How could anyone want to take this to the dump?
OPPOSITE: The refurbished screen.

M
Y SISTER-IN-LAW INHERITED a beautiful Edwardian three-piece screen from her mother. I always coveted it, so when she said that an accident had befallen it and she was going to take it to the dump, I gladly took it off her hands. As you can see from the photograph it was in a pretty sorry state, but the thought of taking it to the dump horrified me and I thought it would make a perfect project for this book.

I'm not suggesting you deliberately vandalise a lovely piece of furniture, but look for a piece that needs to be rescued, a piece that has history but is not antique. Try the saleroom again, this time looking for something more unusual, maybe more ornate. You might find a screen difficult to obtain, (although you can alternatively buy a ready-made screen, but they can be a bit pricey and are often made of very basic materials) so think about other objects such as a chaise-longue or armchair perhaps. The key is to search for the unique. I always think that old furniture has a personality and is definitely either masculine or feminine! Seek out your own ugly duckling that needs a good home. As you will probably have to strip and repair your piece don't make life too difficult; choose one with less textile to be replaced. If you do select an item that has a lot more fabric involved keep it simple, maybe remodel it with something really unusual like towelling and keep embellishment low key.

Even if something is in pieces, like my screen, it's still possible to salvage it, but I will freely admit I have no carpentry skills and will be relying on my husband's expertise to bring it back to life. If you are confident with hammers, saws and nails then

you can select something that poses a real challenge, otherwise think carefully and select distressed rather than dead! You will need to check that anything in pieces has all its component parts: nails and screws are replaceable, missing legs are not. In addition look for woodworm. If the piece appears to be in reasonable condition test out its strength and check its joints. Don't worry too much about garish paint jobs – these can be rectified later and often the nastier the finish the cheaper the piece will be.

I would also suggest, if you have space available, that you buy pieces of furniture as you see them and restore them when you have time. If you don't buy an attractive piece when you see it you won't get a second chance. I have quite a collection now and need to give them some tender loving care fairly soon.

Pieces of furniture waiting to be resuscitated.

Restoring your piece

Providing step-by-step instructions is going to be tricky with this project as we are going to be tackling different pieces. Consequently I'll go through what I plan to do and give information that will be appropriate to whatever you decide to tackle.

The materials I am going to use are: a basic tool kit including hammer, nails, pliers and wood glue, a selection of fabric that works together but does not necessarily match, fabric paints, fabric pens, paintbrushes, tracing paper and pencil, scissors, pins, letter stencil, machine embroidery threads, small sequins, old buttons, self-cover buttons, upholstery tacks and a staple gun (image A).

My screen needs to be reassembled and this is where I shall relinquish it into more capable hands (image B). I'm going to leave the existing

A Some of the equipment needed for this project (see also p.88).

B My husband is fantastic at salvage jobs, here he uses wood glue and clamps to restore the screen.

textile panels in place and cover over them; this will give the new fabric extra strength (image C). You might need to remove the fabric on your piece; this will enable you to use it as a pattern.

Stripping and cleaning

As with the previous project you have to evaluate how much wear your piece is going to have; this will help you decide what fabric to use. As my screen is decorative I'm going to use a combination of reclaimed silk and printed cotton (image D). Silk is wonderful for this type of project, but bear in mind that if furniture is going to be in direct sunlight the fabric will fade and eventually degrade. I am going to make sure that the silk faces away from sunlight. Choose your fabric accordingly.

My next step is to make a pattern, and for this I'm going to trace as accurate a shape as possible from the panels. It's best to use good quality tracing paper for this; you don't want the paper to tear as you are using it. Once the shape has been traced, tidy up the outline so that the shape you translate onto the fabric is neat and accurate. When I draw the shape onto the fabric I will add a small hem allowance (image

C Leaving existing fabric in place will support the new panels.

D A mixture of fabrics will be used for the screen, including some reclaimed silk.

E); I won't need to stitch a hem on the fabric, but the extra fabric will be where I tack the piece onto the screen.

You should aim to cut out all the pieces of fabric you need before beginning any

embellishment, this will enable you to work on all the pieces at once. If you are producing textiles that work as a group it's nice to see them develop together. The final piece will work more effectively, and

E Trace your pattern as accurately as possible, allowing a little extra material for tacking.

F If you can lay out all your pieces together then you will get a better idea of composition and how the new fabric will work.

it's also more time efficient to complete all the painting at the same time, all the stitching at the same time, and so on.

Ideas for embellishment

My pieces of fabric are not that big, and I don't want to overwork them, so I'm going to work out a plan of campaign in my sketchbook. As the screen will be in my sitting-room I want the imagery to work with other items in the room. My room is neutrally decorated so I can use more vibrant colours. I'm not going to use matching fabric in the panels, but the colours work well together and the patterns are chosen for their quirky qualities.

Once you have your fabric cut to size place it on a surface that is big enough for all your shapes. Make sure you protect your table with a cloth as you are going to be using fabric paints and pens. It's a good idea to use a plain white or cream colour cloth as this will allow you to see the colours and decoration more clearly. An old sheet or piece of oilcloth is ideal (image F).

If you have produced some design ideas in your sketchbook this is where you can start translating them onto your fabric. Use an ordinary graphite pencil to draw freehand onto your fabric. Keep your marks light in tone but don't be afraid of making a mistake: you can always stitch or paint over any stray pencil lines. For my project I

The back of the screen.

like the idea of working into the edges of the panels rather than having an all-over design. I like the concept of clusters of intense imagery and decoration. If you overload the decoration the finished piece will be too busy and confused: knowing when to stop is a skill you will develop the more work you produce.

My imagery is based on the marks seen in dress patterns: graphic shapes, arrows and stitch lines. I am also going to include text. Use patterns and shapes that work well with your piece, or the room where the furniture will live (image G). I am also using different fabrics for the front and back of the screen.

Applying decoration

Once you are satisfied with your ideas and have a 'map' to follow, get cracking with your paints and pens. I would point out that unusual pieces of furniture like this screen are not going to be sat on or laundered, so in this case you could use a more unusual medium. Marker pens and biros can be used, as well as glitter glue and acrylic paint. Whatever you decide to work with, test it on a scrap of fabric first. As the image I am using is quite graphic and

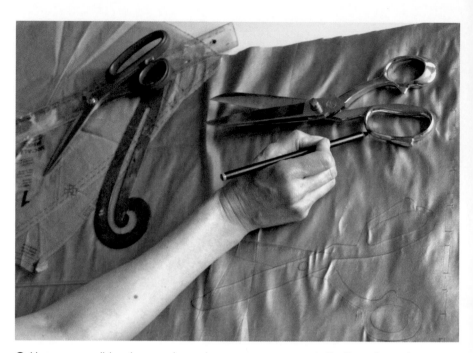

G Use a pencil to draw out any imagery on your cloth. Pencil mark mistakes can be hidden later if necessary.

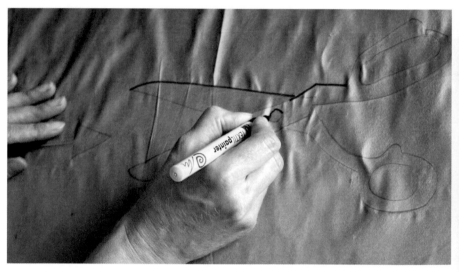

H Fabric pens allow you to achieve lovely linear marks and tidy up the edges of other painted shapes.

linear I am using fabric pens alongside the fabric paints.

Fabric pens

Fabric pens are easily available from your local art shop. They contain dye rather than ink, the dye being fixed by ironing the reverse of the fabric. The pens are very easy to use and work on a variety of fabric weights. I don't use them for their colour, which can sometimes be a bit dull, but they are good when you want to achieve a sharp edge or outline (image H). I am also going to incorporate text in my imagery and the pens are ideal for this.

Using text in a design is a lovely way of creating a personal image; you can include significant names, words or dates. I am using some of the words from the dress patterns that inspired my imagery. In addition to handwriting words I am also going to use stencils.

Stencils and stamps

I bought these plastic stencils years ago from an art shop and they have been used over and over again. I paid about £15 for them which is a bargain considering the years of pleasure they have given me (image I). Stencils like these come in different sizes, but I love the bold scale of the ones I'm using for this project.

You can also buy letter stamps. I have a fantastic collection of wooden typography letters I acquired from my younger brother. They are beautiful to look at and ridiculously expensive if you see them in antique shops. Check out salerooms and internet auction sites for similar ones (image J). You could alternatively use rubber

I   My lovely battered stencils.

J   A collection of old letter stamps.

89

stamps which are quite cheap and easily available. it is possible to have stamps made for you, so if you like a particular pattern or shape and want to repeat it across an area of fabric try ordering some bespoke stamps. Look on the internet for companies offering this service.

Once I have completed the sections of imagery that I am painting and stencilling I am going to leave the paint to dry thoroughly. I will then iron each piece on the back to fix the dye and give me a pristine surface for the next stage (image K).

I'm only going to use small areas of machine embroidery in this project as I'm more interested in applied surface decoration for my screen. However, you might want to go to town with your embroidery. Just remember to use an embroidery hoop to keep the fabric taut – you don't want too much distortion with this project. Think carefully before you use the machine about where you want to apply the embroidery. I am going to work into some of the stencilled letters and emphasise some of the larger shapes.

Sequins and buttons

In terms of applied embellishment I'm going to use small sequins and a mixture of vintage buttons and self-cover buttons. If you decide to use sequins think about using small quantities but applying them densely, so that certain areas of your work twinkle and glimmer. Alternatively, you could apply them in sweeping lines and rows, changing colour as you work. I am using trailing lines across the design, working over the painted areas and text (image L).

When it comes to the final stage of applying more three-dimensional decoration, I want to use different sized self-cover buttons and a selection of old buttons. I am going to continue with the text theme and cover the buttons with fabric that has text all over it. I like the idea of random words catching your eye as you look at the piece. If you are using self-cover buttons try to use fabric that is different in texture or colour from your base fabric: you want to create areas of interest that highlight your imagery

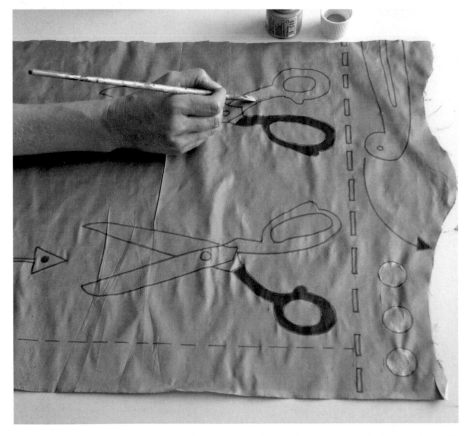

K Paint all the sections of fabric you need and iron them all when they have dried.

or pattern. Consider using multiples of buttons, repeating the decoration across all the panels you are making (image M). I am quite happy with the amount of decoration I have added so am ready to fix the new panels to the screen. Please continue with your decoration if it seems appropriate: it's important that you make something that is personally satisfying.

Tacks and trim

I am using upholstery tacks to fix the fabric to the screen, beginning at the bottom of the panel. As the tacking progresses the fabric will need to be pulled taut across the old fabric – it helps to have a second pair of hands at this point. I repeat the process on each of the panels until I have attached all the fabric (image N).

L The sequins I have chosen are going to work their way across the imagery, not follow its edges.

M Lots of covered buttons work well to give areas of intense colour and pattern.

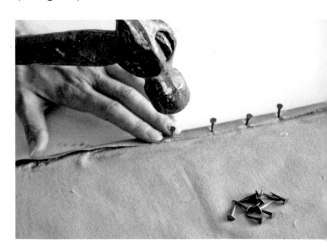

N Find someone to give you a hand when fixing your new fabric, as you want it to be taut.

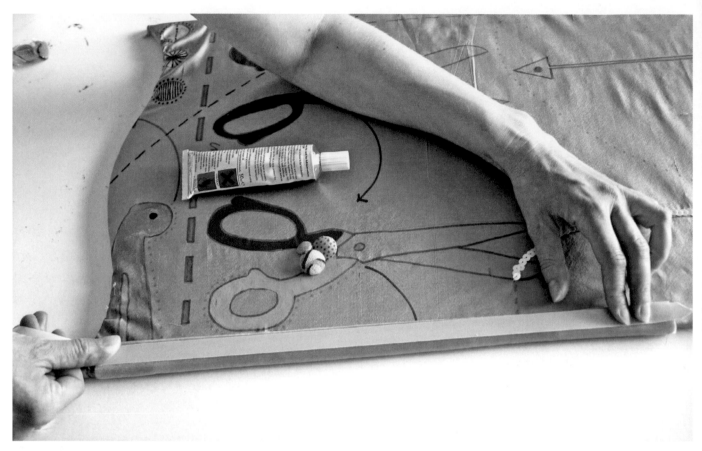

○ Attach your trim carefully and make sure it doesn't have any unfinished edges that will fray.

All the tacks will be visible at this point so you will need to add a trim around the edges. I am using a variety of trims that have been salvaged from clothes, old upholstery and weird lampshades! You can do the same, or to continue with the handmade theme you can make your own trim using leftover ribbon, sequins and buttons. The trim is attached using textile glue. Stick the trim on carefully – don't rush it as you want a professional finish without glue seeping onto your fabric or the piece of furniture. Pay special attention to corners and when you come to the end fold the edges of the trim over so that you achieve a seamless finish that won't fray or unravel (image O).

This has been a difficult project to describe simply because you won't have the same item in front of you as I do, but I hope it will give you the confidence to tackle something similar.

Conclusion

If you have used this book to produce the projects faithfully you should now possess a fine collection of textiles and furniture that has been reworked and revived. What you have made should serve you well, and encourage you to recycle and restore wherever possible. I also think that you should have more confidence with basic sewing skills and applied surface decoration. You don't have to keep these skills for interior textile projects: they can be used equally successfully on clothing, bedding, lighting, in fact wherever there is pre-existing fabric. I hope you view textiles in a different way now and have developed and honed your magpie tendencies!

As with many things what you achieve is often dependent on the time you have to spare. Time is always an issue and often it seems so much easier and less time-consuming to buy new. But you then have what everyone else does, and sometimes a few unique pieces can change an entire room. Time spent on customising objects or reworking them is time well and happily spent; it's also money saved. I can't pretend that it is always possible to reuse every scrap of fabric you possess, and I do invest time and money in sourcing beautiful old textiles and trimmings, but so many items we own are ideal for refashioning into something far more beautiful than you would imagine. For me the key lies in researching and recording; reading magazines for current trends and visiting textile collections. Becoming passionate about themes and objects are all a vital part of the making process. If you can start to develop this enquiring state of mind you will soon find obsessions developing which feed directly into anything you make.

I am including a bibliography, places of interest to visit and suppliers that can all help you to make the most of your skills. Preparation is key; collecting the right equipment and spending time with your fabric will ensure your project looks professional and beautiful. As I said earlier, slow cooking produces intense flavours, and it's the same when working with textiles: if you want sumptuous results then take your time and allow your work to simmer and develop.

Bibliography, Suppliers & Information

Books

Fletcher, Kate; *Sustainable Fashion and Textiles: Design Journeys*, Earthscan Publications, 2008.

Greenlees, Kay; *Creating Sketchbooks for Embroiderers and Textile Artists: Exploring the Embroiderers' Sketchbook*, Batsford, 2005.

Hart, Avril; *North, Susan; Historical Fashion in Detail. The 17th and 18th Centuries*, Victoria & Albert Museum, 2003.

Smith, Paul; *You Can Find Inspiration in Everything – (And If You Can't, Look Again)*, Violette Editions, 2009.

Wolff, Collette; *The Art of Manipulating Fabric*, KP Books, 1996.

Magazines

Selvedge Magazine
Vogue

Collections and places of interest.

The Fashion Museum, Bath.

The V&A Museum, London.

The American Museum, Claverton Manor, Bath.

Snowshill Manor, Gloucestershire. National Trust owned property

Wightwick Manor, West Midlands. National Trust owned property

Liberty, Regent Street, London. Beautiful shop, inspirational products.

The Costume Institute, Metropolitan Museum of Art, New York. An excuse, if one were needed, to visit the most exciting city in the world.

Pitt Rivers Museum, Oxford. Very weird, very wonderful.

Suppliers

UK

The Cloth House
98 Berwick Street, London W1F 0QJ.
47 & 98 Berwick Street, London, W1F 0QJ.
Tel: + 44 (0)207 287 1555
www.clothhouse.com
Beautiful fabrics, unusual leathers and vintage finds.

Donna Flower
www.donnaflower.com
Heavenly vintage fabrics. Also has textile sales at her gorgeous house. Contact Donna for further details.

Jaycotts
Unit D2, Chester Trade Park, Bumpers Lane, Chester CH1 4LT
Tel: 01244 394099
www.jaycotts.co.uk
Internet site and Chester-based shop selling everything to do with machine embroidery and more.

Josy Rose (Online)
Tel: 0845 450 1212
International: +44 207 537 7755
www.josyrose.com
Lovely internet site selling fabulous sequins, beads, and twinkly things.

Sew Essential (Online)
Tel: 01922 722276
www.sewessential.co.uk
Suppliers of Nymo thread and other textile requirements.

MacCulloch and Wallis
25-26 Dering Street, London, W1S 1AT.
Tel: +44 (0)207 629 0311
www.macculloch-wallis.co.uk
Fabrics, trims etc.

USA

Habu Textiles
135 W. 29th Street, Suite 804, New York 10001
Tel: +1 212 239 3546
Japanese and Asian one of a kind textiles and yarns.

Purl
147 & 137 Sullivan Street, New York, NY 10012
Tel: + 212 239 3546
www.purlsoho.com
Patchwork, yarn, fabric and haberdashery.

Brooklyn General Store (Online)
brooklyngeneral.com
Fabrics, yarns, haberdashery etc.

May Arts
www.mayarts.com (Online)
Tel: +1 203 637 8366
US-based ribbon company. They have an opening order of $100 and only sell ribbon by the spool, but it's much cheaper to buy ribbon in bulk and an order from their catalogue will keep you going for ages. Shipping is a doddle and they are friendly and helpful.

Textile events

UK

Contemporary Textile Fair
Landmark Arts Centre, Ferry Road, Teddington, TW11 9NN.
www.landmarkartscentre.org
Selected textile designers and makers show their work.

The Knitting and Stitching Show
Travels to Harrogate International Centre, Alexandra Palace in London and RDS, Dublin.
www.twistedthread.com
Definitive needlecraft event, features commissioned exhibitions and fantastic selection of stitch related retailers.

Art in Action
Waterperry House, Waterperry, Near Wheatley, Oxfordshire, OX33 1JZ.

Tel (information): +44 (0)20 7381 3192
www.artinaction.org.uk
A large fair covering everything, offering a large textile marquee housing makers work and demonstrations.

Origin: the London Craft Fair
Somerset House, Strand, London
WC2R 1LA.
Tel (information): +44 (0)207 806 2500
www.craftscouncil.org.uk
Selected show of approx. 300 makers from all areas of craft, including textiles.

USA

International Quilt Festival
Held in Chicago, Long Beach and
Houston. See website for details.
www.quilts.com/home/shows

Direction (by Indigo)
Metropolitan Pavilion & Altman
Building, 125 West, 18th Street
(between 6th and 7th Avenues),
NY 10011, New York.
www.directionshow.com
Textiles and surface design.

Other avenues

You will need to research your local area for details of salerooms and auction houses. Also worth checking local listings for details of textile fairs.

e bay is absolutely fantastic for sourcing old textiles, trims, fastenings etc; enter key words such as vintage clothing or vintage trimmings and all manner of delights will open up before you!

Please don't forget your local charity shops – tons of potential and you're doing your bit for charity.

Friends and family: raid, beg, steal and borrow! Form a group specifically to swap and exchange not just clothing but interior textiles and objects. Add a bottle of wine and have a great evening.

Index